science for a changing world

Seasonal Distribution and Abundance of Larval and Juvenile Lost River and Shortnose Suckers in Hanks Marsh, Upper Klamath National Wildlife Refuge, Upper Klamath Lake, Oregon: 2007 Annual Report

Annual report of activities performed under Interagency Agreement 04AA204032 in 2007

By Greer O. Anderson, National Oceanic and Atmospheric Administration, Alexander X. Wilkens, Bureau of Reclamation, and Summer M. Burdick and Scott P. VanderKooi, U.S. Geological Survey

Prepared in cooperation with the Bureau of Reclamation

Open-File Report 2009–1014

U.S. Department of the Interior
U.S. Geological Survey

U.S. Department of the Interior
KEN SALAZAR, Secretary

U.S. Geological Survey
Suzette M. Kimball, Acting Director

U.S. Geological Survey, Reston, Virginia: 2009

For more information on the USGS—the Federal source for science about the Earth, its natural and living resources, natural hazards, and the environment, visit http://www.usgs.gov or call 1-888-ASK-USGS. For an overview of USGS information products, including maps, imagery, and publications, visit *http://www.usgs.gov/pubprod*

To order this and other USGS information products, visit *http://store.usgs.gov*

Suggested citation:
Anderson, G.O., Wilkens, A.X., Burdick, S.B., and VanderKooi, S.P. 2009, Seasonal distribution and abundance of larval and juvenile Lost River and shortnose suckers in Hanks Marsh, Upper Klamath National Wildlife Refuge, Upper Klamath Lake, Oregon: 2007 Annual Report: U.S. Geological Survey Open-File Report 2009-1014, 36 p.

Contents

Figures

Tables

Conversion Factors

Inch/Pound to SI

Multiply	By	To obtain
Area		
acre	0.004047	square kilometer (km^2)

SI to Inch/Pound

Multiply	By	To obtain
Length		
centimeter (cm)	0.3937	inch (in.)
millimeter (mm)	0.03937	inch (in.)
meter (m)	3.281	foot (ft)
kilometer (km)	0.6214	mile (mi)
Area		
square kilometer (km^2)	247.1	acre
square meter (m^2)	10.76	square foot (ft^2)
square kilometer (km^2)	0.3861	square mile (mi^2)
Volume		
cubic meter (m^3)	35.31	cubic foot (ft^3)

Temperature in degrees Celsius (°C) may be converted to degrees Fahrenheit (°F) as follows:
$$°F=(1.8×°C)+32.$$
Temperature in degrees Fahrenheit (°F) may be converted to degrees Celsius (°C) as follows:
$$°C=(°F-32)/1.8.$$
Concentrations of chemical constituents in water are given either in milligrams per liter (mg/L) or micrograms per liter (µg/L).

Seasonal Distribution and Abundance of Larval and Juvenile Lost River and Shortnose Suckers in Hanks Marsh, Upper Klamath National Wildlife Refuge, Upper Klamath Lake, Oregon

Annual report of activities performed under Interagency Agreement 04AA204032 in 2007

By Greer O. Anderson[1], Alexander X. Wilkens[2], Summer M. Burdick[3], and Scott P. VanderKooi[4]

Executive Summary

In the summer of 2007, we undertook an assessment of larval and juvenile sucker use of Hanks Marsh in Upper Klamath Lake, Oregon. This 1,200-acre marsh on the southeastern shoreline of the lake represents part of the last remaining natural emergent wetland habitat in the lake. Because of the suspected importance of this type of habitat to larval and juvenile endangered Lost River and shortnose suckers, it was thought that sucker abundance in the marsh might be comparatively greater than in other non-vegetated areas of the lake. It also was hoped that Hanks Marsh would serve as a reference site for wetland restoration projects occurring in other areas of the lake. Our study had four objectives: to (1) examine seasonal distribution and relative abundance of larval suckers in and adjacent to Hanks Marsh in relation to habitat features such as depth, vegetation, water quality, and relative abundance of non-sucker species; (2) determine the presence or absence and describe the distribution of juvenile suckers [35 to 80 mm standard length (SL)] along the periphery of Hanks Marsh; (3) assess spatial and temporal overlap between larval suckers and their potential predators; and (4) assess suitability of water quality throughout the summer for young-of-the-year suckers. Due to the low number of suckers found in the marsh and our inability to thoroughly sample all marsh habitats due to declining lake levels during the summer, we were unable to completely address these objectives in this pilot study. The results, however, do give some indication of the relative use of Hanks Marsh by sucker and non-sucker species.

Through sampling of larval and juvenile suckers in various habitat types within the marsh, we determined that sucker use of Hanks Marsh may be very low in comparison with other areas of the lake. We caught only 42 larval and 19 juvenile suckers during 12 weeks of sampling throughout the marsh. Sucker catches were rare in Hanks Marsh, and were lower than catch rates in other marshes of Upper Klamath Lake and in other nearshore and offshore areas of the lake. Based on the few suckers we did capture in Hanks Marsh, larvae tended to be found more often in vegetated habitats. A modified

---

[1] *greer.anderson@noaa.gov*, National Oceanic and Atmospheric Administration, Yreka, CA
[2] *awilkens@mp.usbr.gov*, Bureau of Reclamation, Klamath Falls, OR
[3] *sburdick@usgs.gov*, U.S. Geological Survey, Klamath Falls, OR
[4] *svanderkooi@usgs.gov*, U.S. Geological Survey, Klamath Falls, OR

sampling design and approach may be necessary to address the objectives in this study, given that declining lake-surface elevation prevented us from adequately sampling all portions of the marsh throughout the sampling season.

Common non-sucker species in Hanks Marsh included juvenile and adult brown bullhead, larval blue chub, tui chub, fathead minnow, and yellow perch. This species composition was similar to that of other marshes in Upper Klamath Lake but most species were found in lower numbers in Hanks Marsh than other marshes. It may be that use of Hanks Marsh is limited by poor water quality, which we found to exist at many sites after June. It also may be that access to or habitat in the marsh is limited at certain times of the year by low water. Although the results from this initial study of Hanks Marsh indicate that the area may have little direct benefit for sucker species, indirect benefits for these species possibly may come from its positive influence on some aspects of water quality in the lake, such as regulation of pH. It also may be the case that use of Hanks Marsh may vary by year and conditions; however, under the current scope of the study, we were unable to investigate inter-annual variability.

Project Introduction and Background

Lost River sucker *Deltistes luxatus* (LRS) and shortnose sucker *Chasmistes brevirostris* (SNS) were listed as endangered by the U.S. Fish and Wildlife Service in 1988. Very little recruitment into the adult population has occurred for SNS since 1997 and for LRS since 2001 (Janney and others, 2007). Poor recruitment may be the consequence of high mortality during juvenile life stages, and several studies focusing on juvenile suckers have reported sharp declines in age-0 catch rates during early fall, as well as extremely low catches of age-1 suckers (Simon and Markle, 2002; VanderKooi and Buelow, 2003; VanderKooi and others, 2006; Hendrixson and others, 2006). These data suggest low recruitment may be caused by an ecological "bottleneck" occurring between the first and second summers of life.

Several hypotheses concerning the causes of poor age-0 to age-1 survivorship have been suggested, including emigration (Harris and Markle, 1991; Gutermuth and others, 2000), poor summer water-quality conditions (Martin and Saiki, 1999), and winter-kill due to low energy reserves during the first fall of life (Foott and Stone, 2005). Emigration, water quality, and winter-kill, however, may all be exacerbated by an underlying lack of suitable in-lake rearing habitat. Likewise, sub-optimal rearing habitat also may restrict juvenile development of energy reserves during summer and fall, which in turn could lead to high over-winter mortality.

The most suitable in-lake habitat for larval suckers is thought to be well-vegetated marsh. Wetlands are not only thought to act as retention areas for larval suckers to reduce emigration from Upper Klamath Lake but Cooperman and Markle (2004) found that emergent macrophytes supported significantly more, larger, and better-fed larvae than submergent macrophytes, woody vegetation, or open water. They also suggested access to emergent macrophytes may be necessary for good year class formation. Additionally, data from The Nature Conservancy (TNC) indicate that larval use of the River Bend marsh was as least as high as use of edge habitats in the Williamson River and higher than use of shore line habitats in Upper Klamath Lake (Crandall and others, 2008). The most suitable in-lake habitat for 35 to 80 mm standard length (SL) (age-0) suckers remains under debate because they have been found in nearshore and offshore habitats, vegetated and non-vegetated habitats, and over a number of different substrates. Although no comprehensive study of age-0 use of marsh habitat in Upper Klamath Lake has been undertaken, access to marsh habitat during summer and fall may be important for age-0 suckers. Recent evidence also suggests that juveniles prefer shallow nearshore habitats and submerged and emergent marsh habitat (Burdick and others, 2008). Marsh habitat available to age-0 suckers in Upper Klamath Lake in the year of this study was composed of the Upper Klamath National Wildlife Refuge and a few sporadic offshore emergent vegetation stands, primarily *Scirpus* species, along the

2

northern and eastern shorelines. This 14,400-acre refuge is composed of the larger Pelican Bay unit in northern Upper Klamath Lake and the smaller 1,200-acre Hanks Marsh unit in southeastern Upper Klamath Lake.

The location of Hanks Marsh, as it relates to lake circulation patterns (Wood and others, 2006), the locations of in-lake spawning grounds (Janney and others, 2007), and large catches of juveniles north and south of the marsh (Burdick and others, 2007), suggests it may be a rearing ground and refuge for larval and juvenile suckers in Upper Klamath Lake. Lake-spawning suckers concentrate their reproductive efforts at the shoreline springs located on the eastern shore of Upper Klamath Lake, immediately north of Hagelstein Park, which is north of Hanks Marsh (Janney and others, 2007). The model of lake circulation presented by Wood and others (2006) suggests lake water in the area of the spawning springs would carry emerging larvae south along the eastern shore towards Hanks Marsh. Therefore, Hanks Marsh may be the first suitable rearing environment that lake-shore spawned larvae encounter. Previous studies indicated evidence of larval and juvenile suckers north and south of Hanks Marsh, which suggest these life stages may be passing through this area and potentially using it as rearing habitat (Burdick and others, 2007). However, prior to this study, the marsh interior had yet to be sampled. If Hanks Marsh provides suitable rearing habitat, it may contribute to juvenile production in the lake.

To determine if Hanks Marsh serves as important rearing habitat for larval and juvenile suckers, we set four main objectives for this study: (1) examine seasonal distribution and relative abundance of larval suckers in and adjacent to Hanks Marsh in relation to habitat features such as depth, vegetation, water quality, and relative abundance of non-sucker species; (2) determine the presence or absence and describe the distribution of juvenile suckers (35 to 80 mm SL) along the periphery of Hanks Marsh; (3) assess spatial and temporal overlap between larval suckers and their potential predators; and (4) assess suitability of water quality throughout the summer for young-of-the-year suckers. While our study was designed to meet these objectives, we were not entirely successful due to unforeseen environmental conditions. Therefore, in this data summary report, we took a mostly descriptive approach.

Methods

Larval Sampling

We investigated the seasonal distribution and relative abundance of larval suckers in Hanks Marsh in Upper Klamath Lake, Oregon (objective 1; fig. 1) by sampling 74 pop net sites and 97 trawl sites during the spring and summer of 2007. Sites were defined as 50×50 m (2,500 m^2) cells, and were randomly selected without replacement from a continuous grid of Hanks Marsh. Grid cells for selection were removed or added when access was restricted or allowed based on lake elevation over the course of the summer. An average of 22 sites were sampled each week with sampling locations occurring at the center of the grid cell based on Global Positioning System (GPS) coordinates, topographic maps, and aerial photographs.

At pop net sampling sites, two paired pop nets were set in close proximity to each other and to the sampling point. Sampling design and protocol was modeled on that of TNC's match net design for sampling four habitat types: (a) 0.5 to 1.0 m deep with vegetation (deep vegetated), (b) 0.5 to 1.0 m deep without vegetation (deep non-vegetated), (c) less than 0.5 m deep with vegetation (shallow vegetated), and (d) less than 0.5 m deep without vegetation (shallow non-vegetated; Hendrixson, 2008). However, due to the nearly uniform depth of the marsh, only two of each of the four habitat types could be sampled at any one site, with a paired design of a vegetated and non-vegetated net set in either deep or shallow water. Sample sites where at least 50 percent of the area enclosed by the pop net contained vegetation were selected to represent vegetated habitats, whereas sites completely devoid of all vegetation were selected to represent non-vegetated habitats. Water depth was measured in the center of each net, and substrate enclosed in the net, distance to nearest vegetation, and distance to nearest shoreline were recorded. This sampling allowed us to describe larval sucker distribution in relation to vegetation, depth, and location in the marsh (objective 1).

Pop nets consisted of two 2.5-cm diameter PVC frames (1.6 × 1.6 m, area = 2.56 m^2), one weighted down with rebar, and the other wrapped in foam to act as a float, with 0.5 m or 1 m tall, 600-μm mesh mosquito netting connecting the two frames to form a cube with an open bottom and top. With this design, we were able to use the nets in dense, emergent or submerged aquatic vegetation, and shallow water. The weighted rebar frame was placed on the bottom, and the float frame was held down with slipknots tied to two opposing corners using a yoke system. Nets were left to soak for at least 30 minutes prior to sampling to allow sample sites to recover from any disturbance caused by setting the net. Nets were triggered remotely by pulling the yoke system, thus releasing the slipknots and allowing the floating frame to rapidly surface. We used small aquarium dip nets to collect every visible fish enclosed in the net, and in areas with macrophytes, we swept the dip nets along the stalks of the vegetation, removing vegetation if necessary to facilitate fish capture. The volume of water within the pop net was swept at least five times after the last fish was captured to ensure no larvae were missed.

Larval suckers also were sampled using a trawl at 97 sites in the marsh between May 7 and July 18 (table 1). This sampling was concurrent with similar sampling conducted by Oregon State University (OSU) in shoreline areas of the Upper Klamath Lake. Our trawl sampling protocol followed methods used by Terwilliger and others (2004), including use of a net of the same design and dimensions, and sampling similar depths and volumes of water. The larval trawl had an opening of 0.8 × 1.5 m with 2.5 m of 1,000-μm Nitex® mesh netting. After waiting 10 to 20 minutes for the area to recover from any disturbance caused by setting the net, the trawl was pulled from 5 to 10 m (mean = 9 m) in water depths of 0.2 to 1.1 m (mean = 0.8 m). One trawl was conducted at each site for a total of 97 trawl samples. Water depth was measured at the beginning and end of each trawl. This sampling allowed us to assess larval sucker distribution throughout Hanks Marsh (objective 1), and compare our catches to catches in other nearshore lake habitats.

Juvenile Sampling

We investigated the use of Hanks Marsh habitat by juvenile suckers (fish greater than 35 mm SL) using 0.9 m diameter hoop-type fyke nets set on the periphery of Hanks Marsh between July 16 and August 14, 2007 (objective 2). Our sampling protocol closely followed the methods used by previous USGS sucker habitat studies, which included overnight sets using nets of the same design and dimensions (see Hendrixson and others, 2006). Hoop-type fyke nets were constructed of 6.4 mm delta mesh with a 0.9 × 4.6 m lead, two 0.9 × 4.6 m lateral wings, five 0.9 m hoops, and two internal fykes. Sets were overnight (20 to 28 hours, mean = 23 hours) in deeper channels and designed to trap 35 mm SL or longer fish. Nets were set between 0900 and 1500 h and pulled between 0800 and 1700 h. Site selection was similar to the larval sampling except that randomly selected 50 × 50 m (2,500 m^2) cells were only selected if they occurred on the periphery of the marsh. An equal number of randomly selected cells different from the larval sampling also were selected from each of four separate areas (Northern Lake-Side, Middle Lake-Side, Southern Lake-Side, and Dike-Side; fig. 1). This allowed us to describe distribution of suckers and potential sucker predators along the marsh edge (objectives 2 and 4). Within each grid cell, sampling sites occurred in deeper channels that provided boat access near the GPS-determined center of the cell. At each sampling site, two nets were set, one facing into the marsh and one facing toward the open water. Water depth was measured at the mouth and lead of each net.

Water Quality and Vegetation

Water-quality data were collected at all pop net, trawl, and fyke net sites, and included water temperature, dissolved oxygen (DO), and pH. This allowed us to describe sucker distribution in relation to these variables (objective 4), and assess the suitability of Hanks Marsh for sucker use. This information was collected instantaneously at each site using a YSI® 600 handheld multimeter water-quality probe. Measurements were taken halfway between the surface and the bottom at the center of pop nets, adjacent to each trawl, and at the mouth of each fyke net. Vegetation species composition and vegetative cover was estimated for each pop, trawl, and fyke net site by visual surveys of each 50 × 50 m site area. Species composition was expressed as a percentage of each of the dominant cover types (*Scirpus spp., Nuphar polysepalum, Typha spp., Polygonum spp., Potamogeton spp., Ceratophyllum spp., Sparganium spp.*, and algal mat). Vegetative cover was estimated based on the percentage of the site area covered in vegetation. For the sake of analysis, trawl and fyke net sampling sites were considered vegetated if they had greater than 50 percent cover and non-vegetated if they had no vegetation.

Protocols for Preserving, Identifying, and Quantifying Fish

For the purpose of species identification, all larval fish were fixed in 5 to 10 percent buffered formalin for 8 to 24 hours and then preserved in 95 percent ethanol. A subset of juvenile suckers (every third fish for a maximum of six fish total) was preserved in 95 percent ethanol in the field for later identification. Preserved larval fish were identified using pigmentation and body shape (D. Simon, Oregon State University, written communication). Because the pigmentation patterns between Klamath largescale suckers *Catostomus snyderi* (KLS) and SNS are similar, we were unable to positively identify larvae of either of these species. Larvae identified as either KLS or SNS were combined and designated as KLS-SNS for the rest of this report. Larval suckers exhibiting intermediate characteristics used to separate LRS larvae from KLS-SNS larvae were designated unidentified sucker larvae. Preserved juvenile suckers were identified to species using a combination of techniques including vertebral counts, lip morphology, and gill raker counts (Markle and others, 2005). Juvenile suckers exhibiting intermediate characteristics were designated unidentified juvenile suckers. All fish were enumerated, and length was measured on larval (notochord length; NL) and juvenile (standard length; SL) suckers to the nearest millimeter. All non-sucker species captured in fyke nets were recorded as members of one of three length classes (small <50 mm, medium 50 to 100 mm, and large >100 mm).

Summarizing and Analyzing Data

We summarized and analyzed data collected from Hanks Marsh based on our objectives and a variety of related questions concerning temporal and spatial abundance and distribution, habitat use patterns, and species composition. For data collected from pop net sampling, we calculated catch per unit effort (CPUE; larvae/m^3). To examine data from larval trawls, we calculated CPUE (larvae/m^3) based on the distance of the haul and the depth of the water (when haul was in water less than the height of the net). We summarized data for larval suckers captured in each gear based on location within the marsh, date, depth, and habitat type (objective 1), by calculating means and standard errors (SE) based on various groupings. In addition, we looked for temporal and spatial patterns in larval sucker distributions. We also examined the interaction between fish length and distribution of larval suckers. Fyke net data for juvenile suckers on the periphery of Hanks Marsh was summarized as CPUE (fish/hour) and was analyzed for temporal, spatial, and habitat specific patterns in abundance and distribution (objective 2). When appropriate, we compared CPUE by habitat types using a Mann-Whitney rank sum test. To describe the size and change in size of larval suckers captured in Hanks Marsh, we regressed average daily sucker length against date. Statistics were calculated using SYSTAT SigmaStat 3.5 software (SYSTAT 2008).

Catch data from pop nets, trawls, and fyke nets in Hanks Marsh were summarized and compared with data from other sites in Upper Klamath Lake and adjacent marshes collected during the summer of 2007. Fish density and species composition data derived from pop net sampling in Hanks Marsh between May 14 and June 20, 2007, were compared with catch data collected from three marshes in the Williamson River Delta over the same time period (Hendrixson, 2008). Trawl CPUE of larval suckers in Hanks Marsh was compared to larval trawl data collected in other nearshore areas of Upper Klamath Lake over the same time period as our sampling (Simon and Markle, 2008). To make this comparison, we converted the data from lakewide trawls (Simon and Markle, 2008) from fish per net to fish/m^3 by using the length of trawls and the dimensions of the trawl opening. Concurrent USGS juvenile sampling in the lake allowed us to compare our juvenile sucker CPUE, sucker length, and sucker species composition from fyke sets in Hanks Marsh to those from trap net sites in Upper Klamath Lake (including nearshore and offshore sites). Although these data were comparable, the net types were slightly different, with trap nets consisting of a 0.6×0.9 m rectangular opening with no lateral wings and fyke nets consisting of a 0.9 m round opening with two lateral wings.

Species composition of all pop net, trawl, and fyke samples in Hanks Marsh was based on the number of individuals of each species (non-sucker and sucker species) captured and was presented as a fractional abundance (number of individuals compared to total catch; objective 3). This total species composition in Hanks Marsh was compared to data collected in nearshore and offshore areas of Upper Klamath Lake (Simon and Markle, 2008; S. Burdick, USGS, written communication, 2007), the Williamson River Delta (Hendrixson, 2008), and the Pelican Bay unit of the Upper Klamath Wildlife Refuge (Mulligan and Mulligan, 2007). Diversity among sites in the lake was compared using a Shannon-Wiener index of diversity (D′) that combines species richness and abundance where:

$$D' = -\Sigma \, p_i \times \ln \, p_i$$

and p_i = proportion of individuals belonging to species i (McCune and Grace, 2002). The standard value of D′ varies between 0 and approximately 4.6 with higher values indicating greater diversity in the community.

Temperature, DO, and pH data were plotted both temporally as well as spatially to look for patterns of water quality in Hanks Marsh. In order to evaluate potential impacts of poor water quality on suckers (objective 4), high and low stress threshold levels were identified based on a review of studies by Loftus (2001). Threshold stress values were defined as follows: temperature (25 °C low stress level, 28 °C high stress level), DO (6.0 mg/L low stress level, 4.0 mg/L high stress level), and pH (9.0 low stress level, 9.75 high stress level). Low stress thresholds are the level of the metric at which suckers are likely to initiate physiologically adaptive responses, whereas high stress thresholds are the point at which adverse sublethal effects are likely to occur (Loftus, 2001). These threshold levels were included in analysis of water quality in the marsh. Comparing water- quality data and sucker distribution provided information about factors influencing use of Hanks Marsh (objective 4).

Results and Discussion

Larval Sucker Distribution and Relative Abundance

We set two pop nets at each of 74 sites in 2007, from which we collected 58 deep vegetated samples, 58 deep non-vegetated samples, 16 shallow vegetated samples, and 16 shallow non-vegetated samples (table 1). We captured 42 larval suckers over the course of 12 weeks of pop net and trawl sampling in Hanks Marsh. Throughout the summer a total of 148 pop nets were set, with set times ranging from 0845 h to 1430 h. Larval suckers were present in 10 percent of pop nets and 16 percent of trawls. Total CPUE of larvae for pop nets was 0.06 suckers/m^3 (0.10 suckers per net) and 0.03 suckers/m^3 for trawl sampling. Large catches were rare with only one pop net and four trawls capturing more than one larval sucker. Larval sucker species composition was 31 KLS-SNS, 5 LRS, and 6 unidentified, or 86 percent KLS-SNS and 14 percent LRS based on the identified portion of sucker catch. Percent composition of sucker species was similar in other larval sampling in marshes of Upper Klamath Lake in 2007, which was 77 percent KLS-SNS and 23 percent LRS (Hendrixson, 2008). Trawl sampling throughout Upper Klamath Lake in 2007 also found a higher percentage of KLS-SNS (97 percent) compared to LRS (3 percent; Simon and Markle, 2008).

Larval sucker NL in Hanks Marsh ranged between 10.0 and 21.5 mm with a mean NL of 15.1 mm (±0.4 SE). Mean NL of KLS-SNS (14.7 mm ± 0.4 SE) was greater than that for LRS (13.8 mm ±1.0 SE). Based on age regressions by Hoff and others (1997), estimated ages were 0 to 85 days (mean = 33 days) for LRS and 13 to 44 days (mean = 24 days) for SNS-KLS. Length of larval suckers captured in Hanks Marsh increased over the summer at an approximate rate of 0.10 mm/d (r^2 = 0.31; fig. 2). There was no clear pattern between length and location within Hanks Marsh, although there did appear to be larger larvae in the interior of the marsh compared with those on the periphery (fig. 3). A Mann-Whitney rank sum test indicated the median length of suckers captured at non-vegetated sites (15.0 mm SL) were approximately the same as those captured in vegetated habitats (14.0 mm SL; p = 0.094 NS). Mean larval sucker lengths in Hanks Marsh (15.1 ± 1.0 mm SL) also were similar to those reported for larval suckers captured in South Marsh (16.1 ± 0.2 mm SL), Goose Bay West (14.7 ± 0.1 mm SL), Goose Bay East (15.3 ± 0.1 mm SL), or other shoreline areas of Upper Klamath Lake (14.8 ± 0.3 mm SL) sampled in 2007 (Hendrixson, 2008; Simon and Markle, 2008).

Larval suckers were found in the marsh between May 10 and July 5 (table 2; fig. 4), but peak catch rates occurred between June 11 and July 5. Spatial patterns of larval CPUE over time within the marsh were difficult to assess because coverage of randomly selected sites was sparse for pop nets and trawls (fig. 5). Declining lake levels over the course of the summer prevented sampling at many sites, with some sites being too deep early in the season and too shallow late in the season to sample. The net result being inadequate spatial and temporal sampling coverage to assess larval patterns of entry and movement and some patterns in habitat use that were originally planned (objective 1). Therefore, further study with set sampling sites in areas of known depth throughout the summer might further clarify if there were patterns present.

Vegetation at sampling sites visited in Hanks Marsh was dominated by *Scirpus* (>58 percent) followed by *Nuphar polysepalum* > *Typha spp.* > *Polygonum spp.* > *Potamogeton spp.* > algal mat > *Ceratophyllum spp.* > *Sparganium spp.* based on visual surveys (fig. 6). At paired pop net sites, the presence of larval suckers was more common in vegetated pop nets (>50 percent vegetative cover) than in non-vegetated pop nets (no vegetative cover). Nine (12 percent) vegetated pop net sites had positive catches for larval suckers versus only five (6 percent) for non-vegetated sites. One site had positive catches in both the vegetated and non-vegetated pop nets.

Due to the nearly level topography in Hanks Marsh and a steady decline in lake surface elevation, the depth of our sampling sites steadily decreased throughout the marsh over time (fig. 7). This created a confounding effect between depth and time on catch rates. For example, all 116 pop net sites sampled prior to July 10 were at least 0.6 m deep and all 32 pop net sites sampled thereafter were less than 0.5 m deep. The nine larval trawl sites that were less than 0.5 m deep were all sampled after July 10. There were no larvae caught in the 32 shallow water (< 0.5 m) pop nets or nine shallow water trawls sampled between July 10 and July 19 (table 2). However, young of the year suckers probably were too large during this time period to be effectively sampled with these gears. The peak larval catch rates occurred at depths between 0.8 and 1.0 m, which took place between early May and late June (fig. 8).

Comparing Hanks Marsh pop net results to other marshes in Upper Klamath Lake, we found that density of larval suckers in the study area was extremely low (fig. 9). Comparing results for an overlapping time period between May 14 and June 20, 2007, west Goose Bay Marsh had the highest density of larval suckers (18.0 suckers per net) followed by South Marsh (9.9 suckers per net), then east Goose Bay Marsh (7.4 suckers per net), then Hanks Marsh (0.10 suckers per net; 0.06 suckers/m^3; Hendrixson, 2008). This difference may be due to input of larvae into the Williamson River Delta marshes from the Sprague and Williamson Rivers, which together likely constitute the largest source of larvae entering Upper Klamath Lake based on estimates of spawning suckers for that river system (Janney and others, 2007). Most larvae in Hanks Marsh, on the other hand, likely originate from spawning populations using springs along the eastern shore of Upper Klamath Lake due to their proximity to these spawning areas and the dominant lake currents during the spring (Wood and others, 2006; Janney and others, 2007). The smaller numbers of larvae in Hanks Marsh could in part be due to a smaller SNS spawning population at the springs spawning area, as was shown for 2006 (Janney and others, 2007), could contribute to lower numbers of larvae immigrating into Hanks Marsh. Shortnose suckers make up a small percentage of suckers spawning on the eastern shore of Upper Klamath Lake, and their larvae tend to be found in higher densities closer to shore than LRS larvae (D. Markle, Oregon State University, oral communication, 2007). Further investigation of the source populations for each marsh area and the movement of larvae in relation to lake currents may better illuminate this point. Another explanation for the low densities of larval suckers could be increased predation in Hanks Marsh. This possibility is discussed in greater detail below.

Hanks Marsh also is low in larval abundance compared to other nearshore habitats in Upper Klamath Lake based on larval trawl data collected during the same period in the summer of 2007 (fig. 10). Larval sucker CPUE (fish/m^3) was highest in trawls within Upper Klamath Lake along the southwest shoreline (2.46) followed by southeast shoreline (1.70), then northern shoreline (1.02), then Hanks Marsh (0.03; Simon and Markle, 2008). The discrepancy between catches in Hanks Marsh to those in other sites along the southeast shore of Upper Klamath Lake suggest that access and use of Hanks Marsh may be limited compared to other nearshore areas of Upper Klamath Lake.

Juvenile Sucker Presence and Distribution

Over the course of 5 weeks of fyke net sampling along the periphery of Hanks Marsh in the summer of 2007, we set a total of 68 nets for a total of 1,629 net hours (table 3), and captured 19 juvenile suckers. Juvenile suckers were present in 20 percent of fyke nets for a mean CPUE of 0.01 fish/hour (± 0.002 SE). Large catches were rare with only 6 percent of fyke nets having more than one juvenile sucker present. Of the six juvenile suckers sacrificed for identification to species, three were identified as SNS, two as LRS, and one was unidentifiable with our methodology. Sparse catches of juvenile suckers made statistical analysis of these data inappropriate and we therefore chose to present a qualitative summary of our results.

We did not note any spatial patterns of juvenile sucker CPUE over time within the marsh. Temporal patterns showed that juvenile suckers occurred on the periphery of Hanks Marsh from July 18 to the end of sampling on August 14 (fig. 11; table 4). The greatest daily mean CPUE occurred on July 18 (0.04 fish/hour), after which it decreased to under 0.02 fish/hour. The number of juvenile suckers caught was inadequate to determine what areas of the marsh or what months of the summer had a higher abundance of juvenile suckers. A qualitative comparison of the four delineated areas show that total CPUE was similar for all areas with Southern Lake-Side (0.012), then Northern Lake-Side (0.009), then Dike-Side (0.008), then Middle Lake-Side (0.005; fig. 12). Fyke net CPUE in vegetated habitats (0.004 fish/hour) was slightly lower than in non-vegetated habitats (0.011 fish/hour). Juvenile sucker catch rates in Hanks Marsh was relatively low compared to nearshore (<100 m from shore) and offshore (>100 m from shore) habitats throughout Upper Klamath Lake sampled during the same period, July 16 to August 14, 2007 (Burdick and others, unpublished data, 2008, fig.13).

Both age-0 and age-1 year classes of juvenile suckers were captured in fyke net sampling in Hanks Marsh. A total of two age-1 suckers were captured, both on July 18 and both measured 104 mm SL. The remaining 17 juvenile suckers were classified as age-0 suckers, based on length-frequency distributions, and were between 40 and 74 mm SL with mean of 52.3 mm (± SE 1.9 mm SL; fig. 14). Subyearling suckers in Hanks Marsh were of a similar length to those captured at other sites in Upper Klamath Lake suggesting it is unlikely that the marsh is used selectively by certain size classes of fish (Burdick and others, unpublished data, 2008).

Spatial and Temporal Overlap between Larval Suckers and Potential Predators

Predation by some non-sucker species on larval and juvenile suckers is an important factor to consider in Hanks Marsh, because predation is considered to be one of the most important factors in mortality of larval fish (Houde, 2002) and may contribute substantially to juvenile sucker mortality. We examined the spatial and temporal overlap between potential predators and suckers (objective 3), but our sampling was not designed to study predator-prey interactions or estimate predation rates. Potential juvenile and larval sucker predators that were found in Hanks Marsh include, brown bullhead *Ameiurus nebulosus*, yellow perch *Perca flavescens*, pumpkinseed *Lepomis gibbosus*, fathead minnow *Pimephales promelas*, marbled sculpin *Cottus klamathensis*, slender sculpin *C. tenuis*, Klamath Lake sculpin *C. princeps*, and largemouth bass *Micropterus salmoides*.

The larval fish community in Hanks Marsh was dominated by native chub species (*Gila spp.*), but non-native and potential predator species were common in our catches. There was a total of six non-sucker species found in pop net and trawl catches for total CPUEs of 0.88 and 0.42 fish/m^3, respectively. Catches from trawls and pop nets were similar in species composition (fig. 15) with the most common species in the combined catch being

blue chub (*G. coerulea*)	50 percent
tui chub (*G. bicolor*)	34 percent
fathead minnow	6 percent
yellow perch	5 percent
marbled sculpin	1 percent
slender sculpin	1 percent

Larval community structure in Hanks Marsh was similar to Goose Bay and South Marshes near the Williamson River mouth (Hendrixson, 2008; fig. 16), with the exception of yellow perch and marbled sculpin larvae which occurred in Hanks Marsh but not the other marshes. While larval fathead minnow, yellow perch, and sculpin species probably do not present a predation threat to suckers, these species are all at least partially picivorous at larger sizes (Moyle, 2002). Total diversity (D') of larval samples, including both non-sucker and sucker species, was 1.26 on a scale from 0.0 to 4.6. The abundance of non-sucker species varied over time with low abundances (<1 fish/m^3) early in the season and later higher catches of species such as tui chub and fathead minnow into June and the first half of July (fig. 17).

Fyke nets caught a greater number of species than larval pop nets or trawls and had higher diversity (D' = 1.36). A total of 17,129 fish from 13 species were caught in fyke nets with the most common being

brown bullhead	57 percent; 5.8 CPUE
tui chub	19 percent; 2.0 CPUE
fathead minnow	10 percent; 1.4 CPUE
yellow perch	5 percent; 0.6 CPUE
marbled sculpin	2 percent; 0.34 CPUE
Klamath Lake sculpin	2 percent; 0.42 CPUE
slender sculpin	1 percent; 0.26 CPUE
pumpkinseed	1 percent; 0.19 CPUE
blue chub	<1 percent; 0.10 CPUE
Largemouth bass	<1 percent; 0.07 CPUE
KLS-SNS, LRS, and lamprey	<1 percent; 0.04 CPUE

A total of 416 fish, or 2 percent of the total catch, was made up of unidentified juvenile sculpin. Based on concurrent USGS juvenile trap net sampling in Upper Klamath Lake, Hanks Marsh has a much higher percentage of brown bullheads (Burdick and others, unpublished data, 2008) but otherwise has a similar species composition (fig. 18). The fish community in Hanks Marsh was less similar to that of Upper Klamath Marsh (Pelican Bay unit of Upper Klamath Wildlife Refuge). Brown bullheads also were common in Upper Klamath Marsh but composed a smaller portion of the overall fish community than in Hanks Marsh (fig. 18). Yellow perch comprised 27 percent of the catch in Upper Klamath Marsh but only 4 percent in Hanks Marsh. The overall diversity in Hanks Marsh was lower than diversity in other areas of Upper Klamath Lake and adjacent marshes with a D' of only 1.36 compared to 1.46 in southern Upper Klamath Lake, 1.51 in northern Upper Klamath Lake, 1.57 in central Upper Klamath Lake, and 1.73 in Upper Klamath Marsh (calculated from data presented by Mulligan and Mulligan, 2007). High catch rates of brown bullhead in Hanks Marsh are likely due to the species' affinity for vegetated areas for spawning and rearing (Sinnott and Ringler, 1987) and may be enhanced by their ability to tolerate low DO and warm temperatures (Moyle, 2002).

The greatest evidence of shared habitat between larval suckers and a potential predator species was with brown bullhead, which occurred throughout the sampling season in shallow vegetated habitats. The median CPUE for juvenile brown bullhead was 1.5 times higher when the entire fyke net lead was placed into vegetation (median 4.05, n = 12) compared to when only part or none of the lead was in vegetation (median 2.63, n = 58). Brown bullheads may prey on larval suckers (Kline and Wood, 1996) but because most of the fish (93 percent) of this species were small (<100 mm) they are not likely to prey on juvenile suckers in Hanks Marsh (mean 52.3 ± SE 1.9 mm SL). Of the potential predator species mentioned above, yellow perch were the largest (20 percent >100 mm SL) and most likely to prey on juvenile fishes between 40 and 100 mm SL, including juvenile suckers (Knight and others, 1984). Peak catch rates for yellow perch of up to 2.6 fish/hour occurred predominantly in July when juvenile suckers were present making predator-prey interaction possible. High fathead minnow catch rates, on the other hand, peaked later in the summer after larval sucker catches had declined to zero, making it unlikely that this species was a dominate predator on larval suckers in Hanks Marsh.

The higher abundance of larval suckers in our vegetated pop net catches suggests that vegetated habitats may provide some refuge from predation in Hanks Marsh, despite the spatial and temporal overlap with brown bullheads. In laboratory studies, Markle and Dunsmoor (2007) demonstrated that depth and vegetation provided larval suckers with some refuge from predation. Therefore, predation in shallow water might be especially important when lake levels decline and the abundance of vegetated refuge habitat is diminished. In low water, predation on larvae also may be higher due to increased density of predators.

Water Quality

Poor water quality may have sublethal effects on juvenile suckers in Hanks Marsh (Loftus, 2001; Terwilliger and others, 2003). To assess these effects, we compared conditions known to elicit stress responses in suckers with conditions in Hanks Marsh. These thresholds were based on a review of past studies by Loftus (2001) and included both low stress thresholds and those that likely result in sublethal effects (high stress threshold). Both low and high stress thresholds of temperature, DO, and pH were exceeded at some sites in Hanks Marsh during our sampling and median daily values for the marsh exceeded stress levels for temperature and DO at least once during the summer (fig. 19). Temperature generally increased between April and July, with low stress threshold levels reached at numerous sites toward the end of June and high stress thresholds exceeded at one site on July 16. Median daily temperature exceeded low stress thresholds on the same day. Dissolved oxygen showed similar patterns of decreasing water quality over the course of the summer, with DO low stress threshold levels exceeded in May and another five times before the end of sampling in July. High DO stress levels were exceeded at many individual sites in July. Although median levels of pH never exceeded stress thresholds in the marsh, levels of pH exceeded low stress levels (9.00) at 3 percent of sites sampled in June and at 12 percent of sites sampled in July. High stress levels of pH (9.75) were only exceeded once at one site on July 9.

Daily median temperature was similar between the Upper Klamath Lake and Hanks Marsh until June 26. After that, the median difference in daily median temperatures was 1.23 °C warmer in Hanks Marsh than the rest of the lake. This is likely due to the shallowness of and a lack of water exchange in Hanks Marsh, especially as lake surface elevation declined. Compared with lakewide trends in daily median values recorded at 14 sites throughout the lake during the summer of 2007 (M. Lindenburg, U.S. Geological Survey, unpublished data, 2007), median pH was lower in Hanks Marsh after May 26 and median DO generally was lower after June 6 (fig. 19). Comparing the median differences after May 26, the daily median DO was 1.99 mg/L lower in Hanks Marsh than the rest of the lake, and after June 6, the daily median pH was 1.35 units lower in Hanks Marsh than the rest of the lake. Spatial patterns in water quality within the marsh indicated that DO and pH were lower at interior sites than sites on the periphery during two periods (May 17 to June 5 and June 26 to July 12; fig. 19).

In Upper Klamath Lake, DO concentrations are negatively correlated with cool spring temperatures, but as water temperature rises in the summer, trends in both pH and DO are better explained by the dynamics of *Aphanizomenon flos aquae* (AFA) blooms (Wood and others, 2006). The massive blooms of AFA, common in Upper Klamath Lake, were not observed in Hanks Marsh in 2007, which may partially explain differences in June and July water quality between the two areas. Instead, the water in Hanks Marsh had a brownish color that is indicative of high dissolved organic carbon (DOC; Ishikawa and others, 2006). It is possible that AFA was controlled by humic acid, which is commonly found at elevated concentrations in marshes (Peek, 1963). At DOC concentrations less than 15 mg/L, there is a strong negative correlation with pH (Ishikawa and others, 2006), which may partially explain why pH typically was lowest in the interior of Hanks Marsh.

Of the previously mentioned parameters, Martin and Saiki (1999) found that DO is the most critical factor affecting juvenile Lost River sucker survival in Upper Klamath Lake. Therefore, while Hanks Marsh may have buffered swings in pH, this probably did not substantially affect sucker survival. Previous studies indicate that suckers tend to avoid areas of low DO, and that high temperatures (>22 °C) coupled with low DO tend to reduce growth rates of suckers (Terwilliger and others, 2003; 2004). Therefore, the concentrations of DO that we recorded in May were likely adequate for the survival and growth of larval suckers. However, it is possible that low DO in Hanks Marsh may limit use or inhibit growth by juvenile suckers in June and July. Further studies into the relations among water quality, use of marshes such as Hanks Marsh, and the performance of juvenile suckers inhabiting the marsh could more directly answer this question.

Summary

The results of this pilot study indicate that larval and juvenile sucker use of Hanks Marsh may be very low. Three separate age classes of suckers (larvae, age-0, and age-1) were present in the marsh although abundance of age-1 suckers (2) and age-0 suckers (17) in our catches was minimal. Within the marsh, larval suckers were more commonly caught in vegetated habitats than non-vegetated open water areas. Overall abundance of larval suckers was substantially lower in Hanks Marsh than in other marsh and open water sites in Upper Klamath Lake in 2007. Non-sucker larval species composition, however, was similar to other marsh sites in the lake. It is possible that the high number of potential predators such as brown bullhead and yellow perch found in Hanks Marsh may limit larval and juvenile sucker abundance through predation. Low DO concentrations in June and July also may limit the suitability of Hanks Marsh as habitat for juvenile suckers. Although the results of this initial study indicate that seasonal use of Hanks Marsh by larval and juvenile suckers may be low, this area may play an important role as overwintering habitat for suckers, influence food webs used by suckers (for example, as a source of macrodetritus organic matter or invertebrate production), or help regulate pH in Upper Klamath Lake. It also is important to keep in mind that use of Hanks Marsh by young-of-the-year suckers may vary annually depending on different environmental conditions in the lake or levels of larval production. The current study was not designed to capture such variability. Further research in Hanks Marsh should be designed to: (1) capture the effects of interannual variation in environmental conditions, (2) understand predator-prey interactions, and (3) gain a better understanding of how the marsh influences water chemistry in Upper Klamath Lake.

Acknowledgments

We thank Darin Taylor, Mark Johnson, Missy Braham, and Anna Willard for help with data collection and Kevin Donner, Matt Abel, and Dave Simon (Oregon State University) for help with sucker species identification. Dave Simon also provided data for comparison along with Heather Hendrixson (The Nature Conservancy). We also thank Greta Blackwood for help with database development and management. This work was funded by the Bureau of Reclamation (Interagency Agreement 04AA204032) and the U.S. Geological Survey.

References Cited

Burdick, S.M., Wilkens, A.X., and VanderKooi, S.P., 2007, Nearshore and off-shore habitat use by endangered, juvenile Lost River and shortnose suckers in Upper Klamath Lake, Oregon: 2006 Data Summary: Report of U.S. Geological Survey, Western Fisheries Research Center, Klamath Falls Field Station to Bureau of Reclamation, Mid-Pacific Region, Klamath Falls, Oregon.

Burdick, S.M., Hendrixson, H.A., and VanderKooi, S.P., 2008, Age-0 Lost River sucker and shortnose sucker nearshore habitat use in Upper Klamath Lake, Oregon: A patch occupancy approach: Transactions of the American Fisheries Society, v. 137, no. 2, p. 417-431.

Cooperman, M.S., and Markle, D.F., 2004, Abundance, size, and feeding success of larval shortnose suckers and Lost River suckers from different habitats of the littoral zone of Upper Klamath Lake: Environmental Biology of Fishes, v. 71, p. 365-377.

Crandall, J.D., Bach, L.B., Rudd, N., Stern, M., and Barry, M., 2008, Response of larval Lost River and shortnose suckers to wetland restoration at the Williamson River Delta, Oregon: Transactions of the American Fisheries Society, v. 137, p. 402-416.

Foott, J.S., and Stone, R., 2005, Bio-energetic and histological evaluation of juvenile (0+) sucker fry from Upper Klamath Lake collected in August and September 2004: FY2004 Report from U.S. Fish and Wildlife Service California-Nevada Fish Health Center, Anderson, California.

Gutermuth, B., Pinkston, E., and Buettner, M., 2000, A-canal fish entrainment 1997 and 1998 with emphasis on endangered suckers: Report of New Earth/Cell Tech to U.S. Fish and Wildlife Service, Klamath Falls, Oregon.

Harris, P.M., and Markle, D.F., 1991, Quantitative estimates of fish transported from Upper Klamath Lake through A-canal, Klamath project: Report of Oregon State University to Bureau of Reclamation, Klamath Falls, Oregon.

Hendrixson, H.A., 2008, Non-native fish species and Lost River and shortnose suckers use of restoration and undisturbed wetlands at the Williamson River Delta: Final report for activities conducted in 2006 and 2007: Report of The Nature Conservancy, Klamath Falls to U.S. Fish and Wildlife Service, Ecosystem Restoration Office, Klamath Falls, Oregon.

Hendrixson, H.A., Herring, B.L., Burdick, S.M., and VanderKooi, S.P., 2006, Nearshore and offshore habitat use by endangered, juvenile Lost River and shortnose suckers in Upper Klamath Lake, Oregon. Annual Report 2004: Report of U.S. Geological Survey, Western Fisheries Research Center, Klamath Falls Field Station to Bureau of Reclamation, Mid-Pacific Region, Klamath Falls, Oregon.

Hoff, G.R., Logan, D.J., and Markle, D.F., 1997, Otolith morphology and increment validation in young Lost River and shortnose suckers: Transactions of the American Fisheries Society, v.126, p. 488-494.

Houde, E.D., 2002, Mortality, in Fuiman, L.A., and Werner, R.G., eds., Fishery science: The unique contribution of early life stages: Oxford, UK, Blackwell Scientific Publications, p. 64-87.

Ishikawa, T., Yurenfrie, Ardianor, and Gumiri, S., 2006, Dissolved organic carbon concentration of a natural water body and its relationship to water color in Central Kalimantan, Indonesia: Limnology, v. 7, p. 143-146.

Janney, E.C., Barry, P.M., Hayes, B.S., Shively, R.S., and Scott, A.C., 2007, Demographic analysis of adult Lost River suckers and shortnose suckers in Upper Klamath Lake and its tributaries, Oregon 2006: Report of U.S. Geological Survey, Western Fisheries Research Center, Klamath Falls Field Station to Bureau of Reclamation, Mid-Pacific Region, Klamath Falls, Oregon.

Kline, J.L., and Wood, B.M., 1996, Food habits and diet selectivity of the brown bullhead: Journal of Freshwater Ecology, v. 11, p. 145-151.

Knight, R.L., Margraf, F.J., and Carline, R.T., 1984, Piscivory by walleye and yellow perch in western Lake Erie: Transactions of the American Fisheries Society, v. 113, p. 677-693.

Loftus, M.E., 2001, Assessment of potential water quality stress to fish: Report of R2 Resource Consultants, Inc. to Bureau of Indian Affairs, Portland, Oregon.

McCune, B., and Grace, J.B., 2002, Analysis of Ecological Communities: Mjm publishing, Gleneden, Oregon.

Martin, B.A., and Saiki, M.K., 1999, Effects of ambient water quality on the endangered Lost River sucker in Upper Klamath Lake, Oregon: Transactions of the American Fisheries Society, v. 128, p. 953-961.

Markle, D.F., and Dunsmoor, L.K., 2007, Effects of habitat volume and fathead minnow introductions on larval survival of two endangered sucker species in Upper Klamath Lake, Oregon: Transactions of the American Fisheries Society, v. 136, p. 567-579.

Markle, D.F., Cavalluzzi, M.R., and Simon, D.C., 2005, Morphology and taxonomy of Klamath Basin suckers (Catostomidae): Western North American Naturalist, v. 65, p. 473-489.

Moyle, P.B., 2002, Inland fishes of California: 2nd edition, University of California Press: Berkeley, California.

Mulligan, T.J., and Mulligan, H.L., 2007, Habitat utilization and life history of fishes in Upper Klamath National Wildlife Refuge Marsh, Fourmile Creek and Odessa Creek, Oregon: Report of Humboldt State University to Bureau of Reclamation, Klamath Falls, Oregon.

National Research Council (NRC), 2004, Endangered and threatened fishes in the Klamath River Basin: The National Academics Press, Washington, DC.

Peek, C.A., 1963, The humic water of Klamath Marsh and its effect on the growth of *Anabaena Cylindrica* Lemm. in culture: Corvallis, Oregon State University, Ph.D. dissertation.

Simon, D.C., and Markle, D.F., 2002, Ecology of Upper Klamath Lake shortnose and Lost River suckers, Annual survey of abundance and distribution of age-0 shortnose and Lost River suckers in Upper Klamath Lake, 2001 Annual Report: Report of Oregon Cooperative Research Unit, Department of Fisheries and Wildlife, Oregon State University to U.S. Geological Survey, Corvallis, Oregon and Klamath Project, Bureau of Reclamation, Klamath Falls, Oregon.

Simon, D.C., and Markle, D.F., 2008, Ecology of Upper Klamath Lake shortnose and Lost River suckers, Annual survey of abundance and distribution of age-0 shortnose and Lost River suckers in Upper Klamath Lake, 2007 Annual Report: Report of Oregon Cooperative Research Unit, Department of Fisheries and Wildlife, Oregon State University to U.S. Geological Survey, Corvallis, Oregon, and Klamath Project, Bureau of Reclamation, Klamath Falls, Oregon.

Sinnott, T.J., and Ringler, N.H., 1987, Population biology of the brown bullhead (*Ictalurus nebulosus* Lesueur): Journal of Freshwater Ecology, v. 4, p. 225-234.

SYSTAT, 2008, SigmaPlot 11 User's Guide: SigmaStat Press, San Jose, CA.

Terwilliger, M.R., Markle, D.F., and Kann, J., 2003, Associations between water quality and daily growth of juvenile shortnose and Lost River suckers in Upper Klamath Lake, Oregon: Transactions of the American Fisheries, v. 132, p. 691-708.

Terwilliger, M.R., Simon, D.C., and Markle, D.F., 2004, Larval and juvenile ecology of Upper Klamath Lake suckers: 1998–2003: Final report of Oregon State University to Bureau of Reclamation, Klamath Falls, Oregon.

VanderKooi, S.P., and Buelow, K.A., 2003, Nearshore habitat use by endangered juvenile suckers in Upper Klamath Lake, Oregon, Annual Report 2001: Report of U.S. Geological Survey, Western Fisheries Research Center, Klamath Falls Field Station to Bureau of Reclamation, Mid-Pacific Region, Klamath Falls, Oregon.

VanderKooi, S.P., Hendrixson, H.A., Herring, B.L., and Coshow, R.H., 2006, Nearshore habitat use by endangered juvenile suckers in Upper Klamath Lake, Oregon, Annual Report 2002 – 2003: Report of U.S. Geological Survey, Western Fisheries Research Center, Klamath Falls Field Station to Bureau of Reclamation, Mid-Pacific Region, Klamath Falls, Oregon.

Wood, T.M., Hoilman, G.R., and Lindenberg, M.K., 2006, Water quality conditions in Upper Klamath Lake, Oregon 2002-2004: U.S. Geological Survey Scientific Investigations Report 2006-5209, 52 p.

Table 1. Number of pop nets and trawls set each week in Hanks March, Upper Klamath Lake, Oregon, 2007.

[Each pop net site, either deep or shallow, was sampled with a pair of nets. One net was set in a non-vegetated area and one in a vegetated area. Habitat classes are based on the percentage of vegetative cover (non-vegetated = 0 percent and vegetated > 50 percent) and depth (shallow ≤ 0.5 m and deep > 0.5 m). Trawls were taken throughout the marsh between 0.2 and 1.1 m depth in all habitat types]

Week	Pop Nets					Trawls
	Non-Vegetated Deep	Vegetated Deep	Non-Vegetated Shallow	Vegetated Shallow	Total Pop Nets	Total Trawls
30-Apr	9	9	–	–	18	0
7-May	7	7	–	–	14	9
14-May	8	8	–	–	16	11
21-May	3	3	–	–	6	4
28-May	2	2	–	–	4	9
4-June	6	6	–	–	12	8
11-June	6	6	–	–	12	10
18-June	7	7	–	–	14	9
25-June	6	6	–	–	12	8
2-July	4	4	–	–	8	10
9-July	–	–	8	8	16	11
16-July	–	–	8	8	16	8
Total	58	58	16	16	148	97

Table 2. Mean catch per unit effort for pop net catches (larval suckers per net) and trawls (larval suckers per m^3) in Hanks Marsh, Upper Klamath Lake, Oregon, 2007.

[Habitat classes are based on the percentage of vegetative cover (non-vegetated = 0 percent and vegetated >50 percent) and depth (shallow ≤ 0.5 m and deep >0.5 m). Trawls were taken throughout the marsh between 0.2 and 1.1 m depth in all habitat types. Standard errors (SE) are given in parentheses]

Week	Pop Nets					Trawls
	Non-Vegetated Deep	Vegetated Deep	Non-Vegetated Shallow	Vegetated Shallow	Total Pop Nets	Total Trawls
30-Apr	0	0	-	-	0	0
7-May	0	0.14 *(0.06)*	-	-	0.07 *(0.07)*	0
14-May	0	0.25 *(0.13)*	-	-	0.13 *(0.08)*	0
21-May	0.33 *(0.19)*	0	-	-	0.17 *(0.17)*	0.04 *(0.04)*
28-May	0	0	-	-	0	0.03 *(0.02)*
4-June	0.17 *(0.10)*	0.17 *(0.10)*	-	-	0.17 *(0.11)*	0.04 *(0.02)*
11-June	0	0.83 *(0.35)*	-	-	0.41 *(0.25)*	0.02 *(0.01)*
18-June	0.14 *(0.10)*	0.14 *(0.10)*	-	-	0.14 *(0.09)*	0.02 *(0.01)*
25-June	0.33 *(0.19)*	0	-	-	0.17 *(0.11)*	0.07 *(0.06)*
2-July	0	0.5	-	-	0.25 *(0.16)*	0.1 *(0.05)*
9-July	-	-	0	0	0	0
16-July	-	-	0	0	0	0
Total	0.07 *(0.03)*	0.16 *(0.05)*	0	0	0.11 *(0.03)*	0.03 *(0.01)*

Table 3. Number of fyke nets set each week in Hanks Marsh, Upper Klamath Lake, Oregon, 2007.

[Fyke nets were set in pairs with opposite orientation at four different areas of the marsh (see fig. 1 for area boundaries)]

Week	Fyke Nets				
	Northern Lake-Side	Middle Lake-Side	Southern Lake-Side	Dike-Side	Total
16-July	2	2	2	0	6
23-July	4	4	4	4	16
30-July	4	4	4	2	14
6-Aug	4	4	4	4	16
13-Aug	4	4	4	4	16
Total	18	18	18	14	68

Table 4. Mean catch per unit effort (juvenile suckers per hour) for juvenile fyke nets set each week in Hanks Marsh, Upper Klamath Lake, Oregon, 2007.

[Fyke nets were set in pairs with opposite orientation at four different areas of the marsh (see fig. 1 for area boundaries). Standard errors (SE) are given in parentheses]

Week	Fyke Nets				
	Northern Lake-Side	Middle Lake-Side	Southern Lake-Side	Dike-Side	Average
16-July	0	0	0.04 *(0)*	-	0.01 *(0)*
23-July	0.02 *(0)*	0.02 *(0.01)*	0	0	0.01 *(0)*
30-July	0	0	0.02 *(0)*	0	0.01 *(0)*
6-Aug	0.02 *(0.01)*	0	0.02 *(0.01)*	0.02 *(0.01)*	0.02 *(0.01)*
13-Aug	0.02 *(0.01)*	0	0.02 *(0.01)*	0.02 *(0.01)*	0.02 *(0.01)*
Total	0.01 *(0.02)*	0.00 *(0.01)*	0.02 *(0.02)*	0.01 *(0.01)*	0.01 *(0.03)*

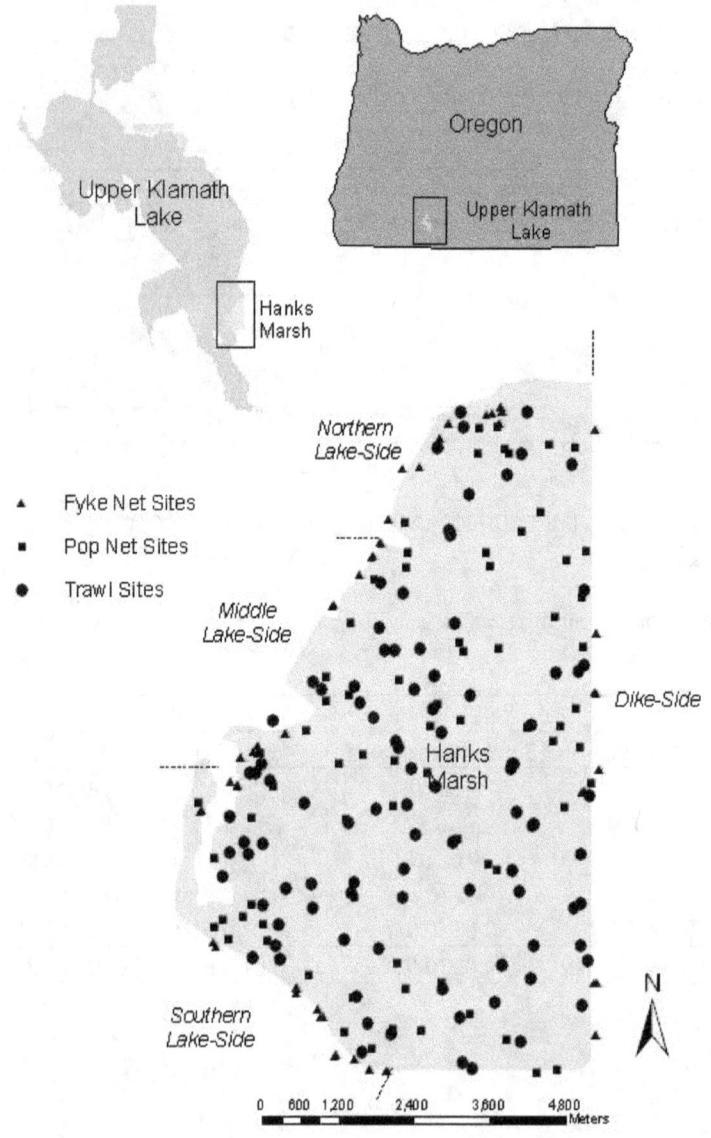

Figure 1. Map of sampling locations by gear type in Hanks Marsh, Upper Klamath Lake, Oregon, during the summer of 2007. Four periphery sampling areas are shown; Northern Lake-Side, Middle Lake-Side, Southern Lake-Side, and Dike-Side.

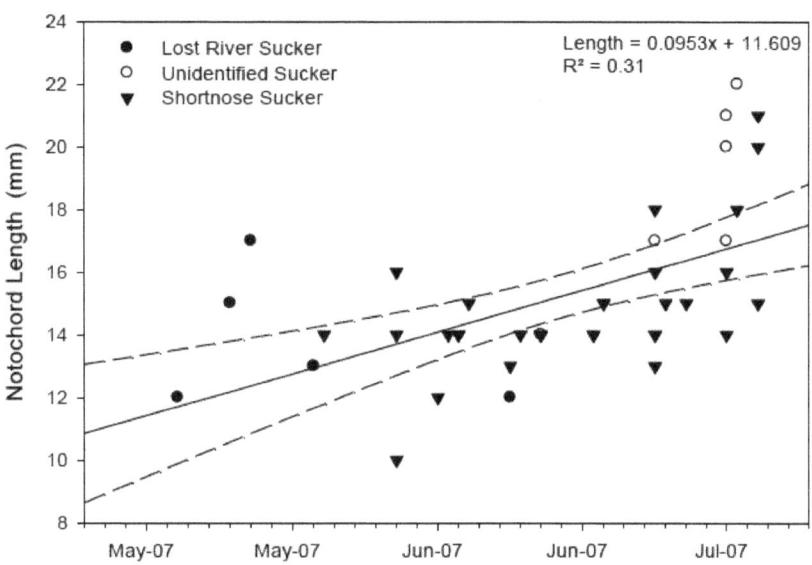

Figure 2.   Notochord length (mm) for larval suckers captured by pop nets and trawls between May 9 and July 5, 2007, in Hanks Marsh, Upper Klamath Lake, Oregon. A regression based on all three sucker species categories (Lost River, shortnose, or unidentified) combined and appropriate 95-percent confidence intervals also is included along with the regression equation and fit (R^2) of the data.

Figure 3.   Mean notochord length (mm) of larval suckers at pop net and trawl sites in Hanks Marsh, Upper Klamath Lake, Oregon, April 30 to July 19, 2007. Data from a total of 42 sites is shown.

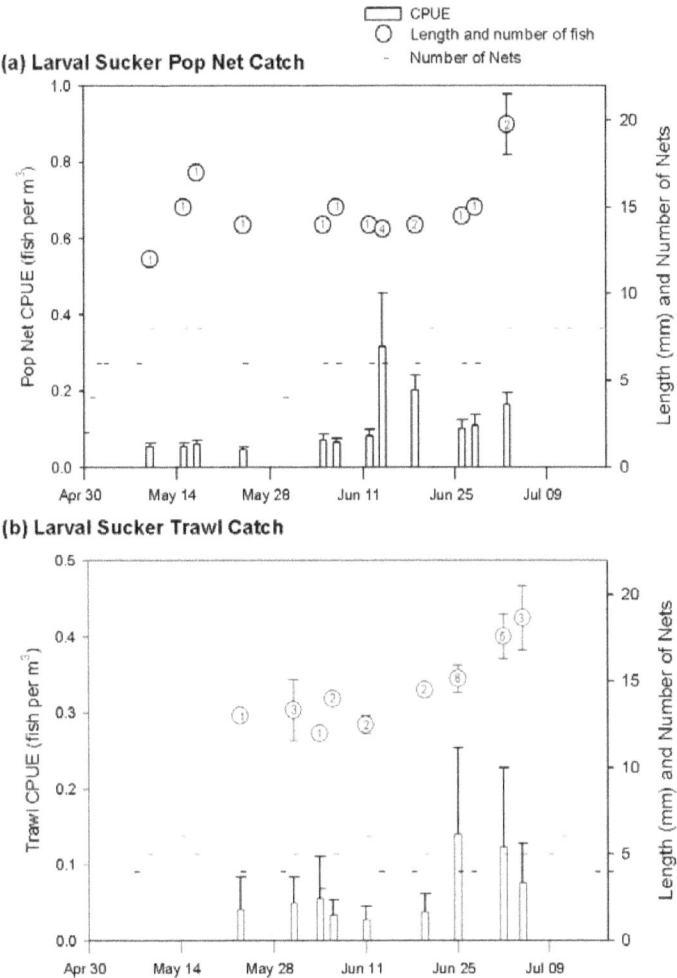

Figure 4. Mean daily catch per unit effort (CPUE) and mean notochord length (mm; + 1 SE) for larval suckers captured between April 30 and July 19, 2007 in (a) pop nets, and (b) trawls in Hanks Marsh, Upper Klamath Lake, Oregon. Sample sizes used to calculate mean CPUEs and lengths are given.

(a) Pop Nets

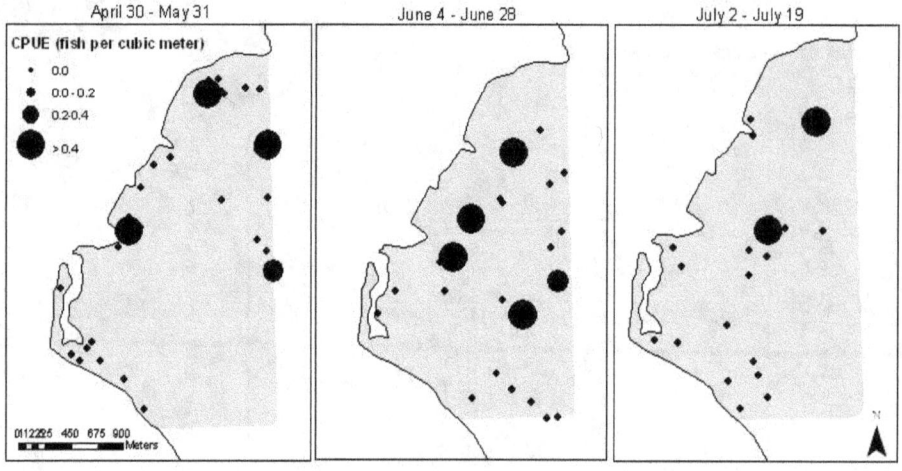

(b) Trawls

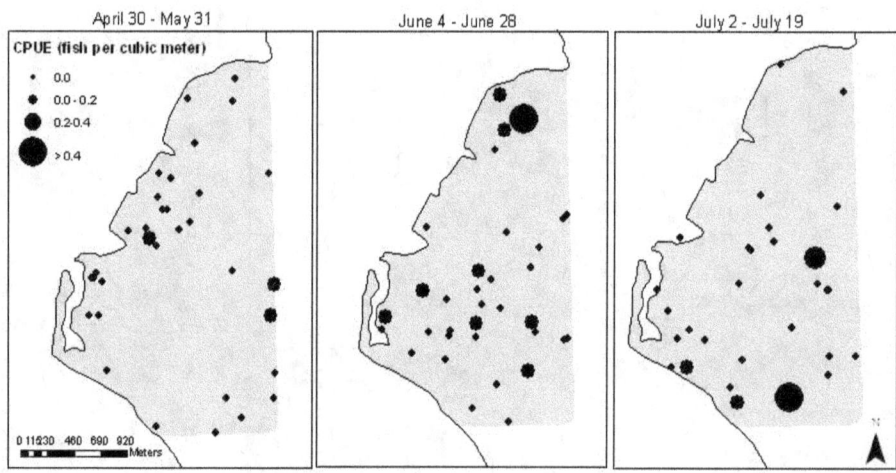

Figure 5. Catch per unit effort (CPUE; larvae per m^3) of larval suckers at (a) pop net and (b) trawl sites over 3 months between April 30 and July 19, 2007 in Hanks Marsh, Upper Klamath Lake, Oregon.

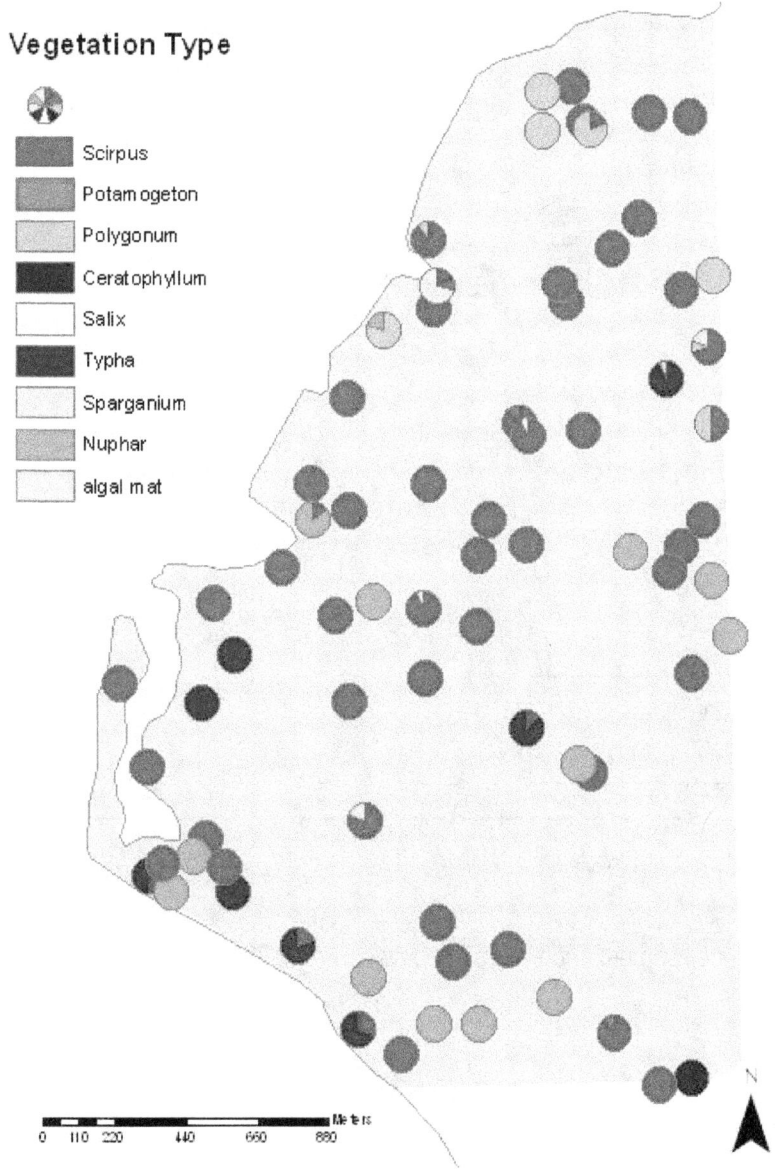

Figure 6. Vegetation types (percent cover by genus) at pop net sites visited in Hanks Marsh, Upper Klamath Lake, Oregon, 2007.

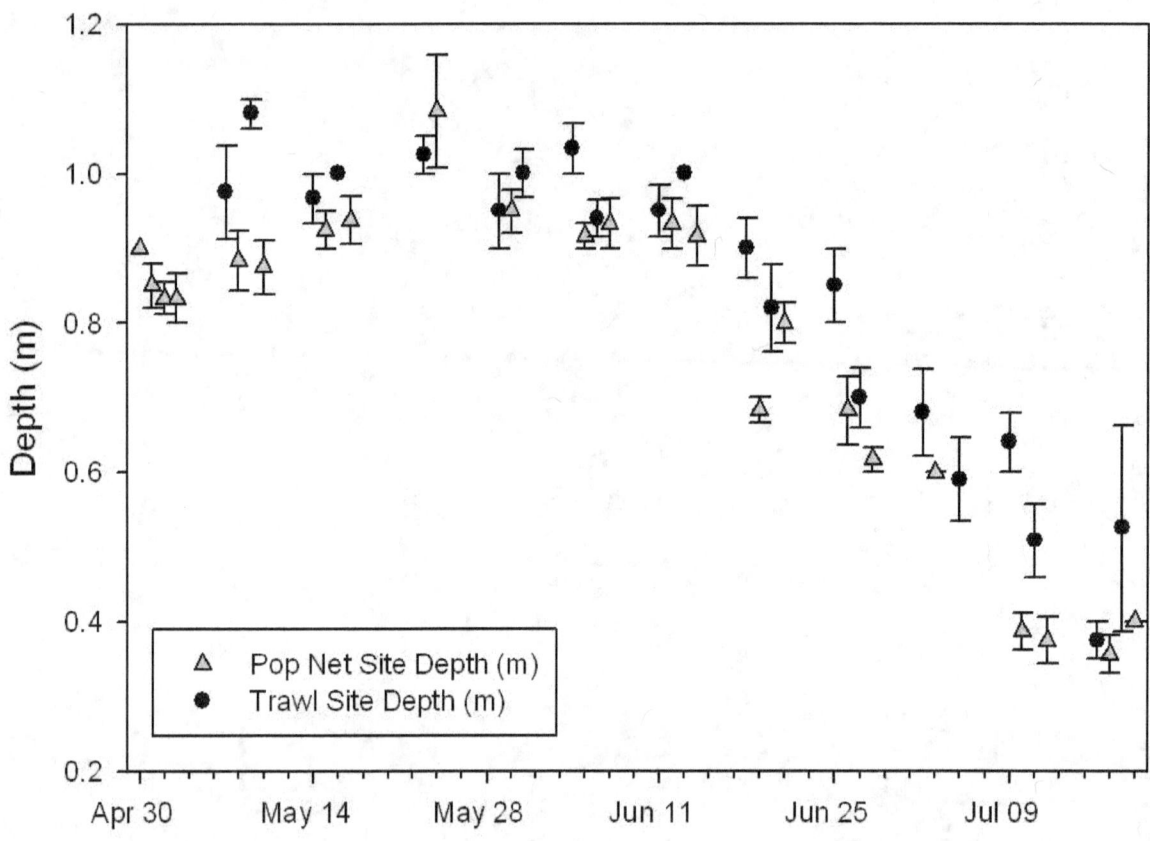

Figure 7.   Mean depths (± 1 SE) for pop net and trawl sites between April 30 and July 19, 2007, in Hanks Marsh, Upper Klamath Lake, Oregon.

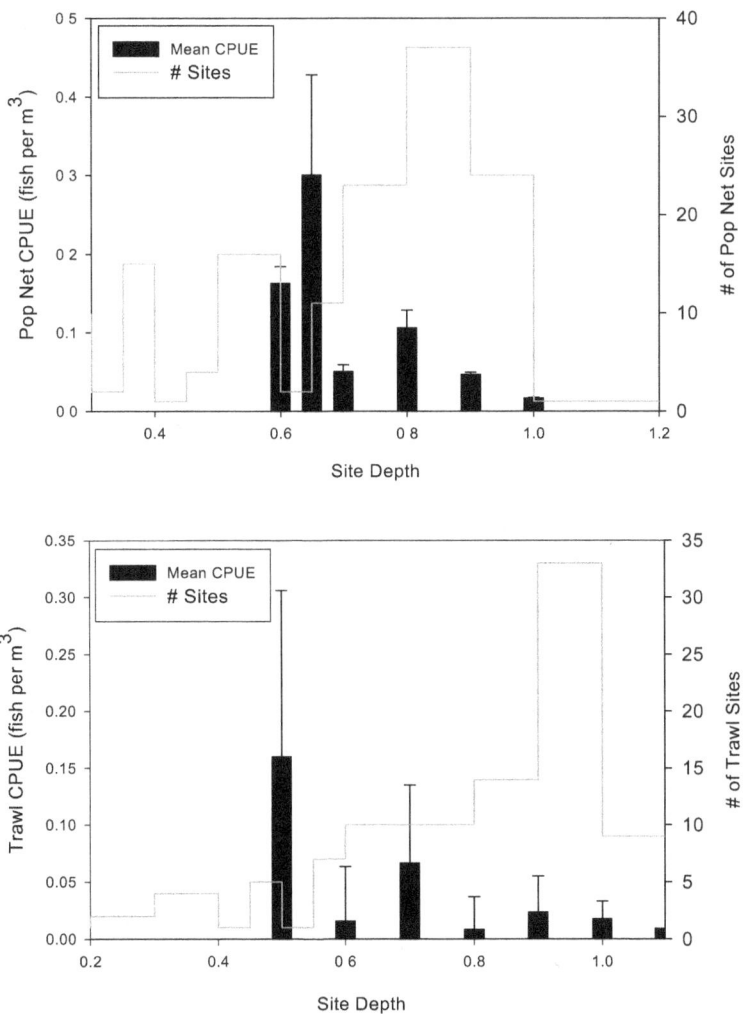

Figure 8. Mean juvenile sucker catch per unit effort (CPUE; fish per m³; + 1 SE) by (a) pop nets and (b) trawls based on site depth (m) in Hanks Marsh, Upper Klamath Lake, Oregon. The number of sites sampled at each depth also is included. Pop nets were set between April 30 and July 19 and trawls were fished between May 7 and July 18, 2007.

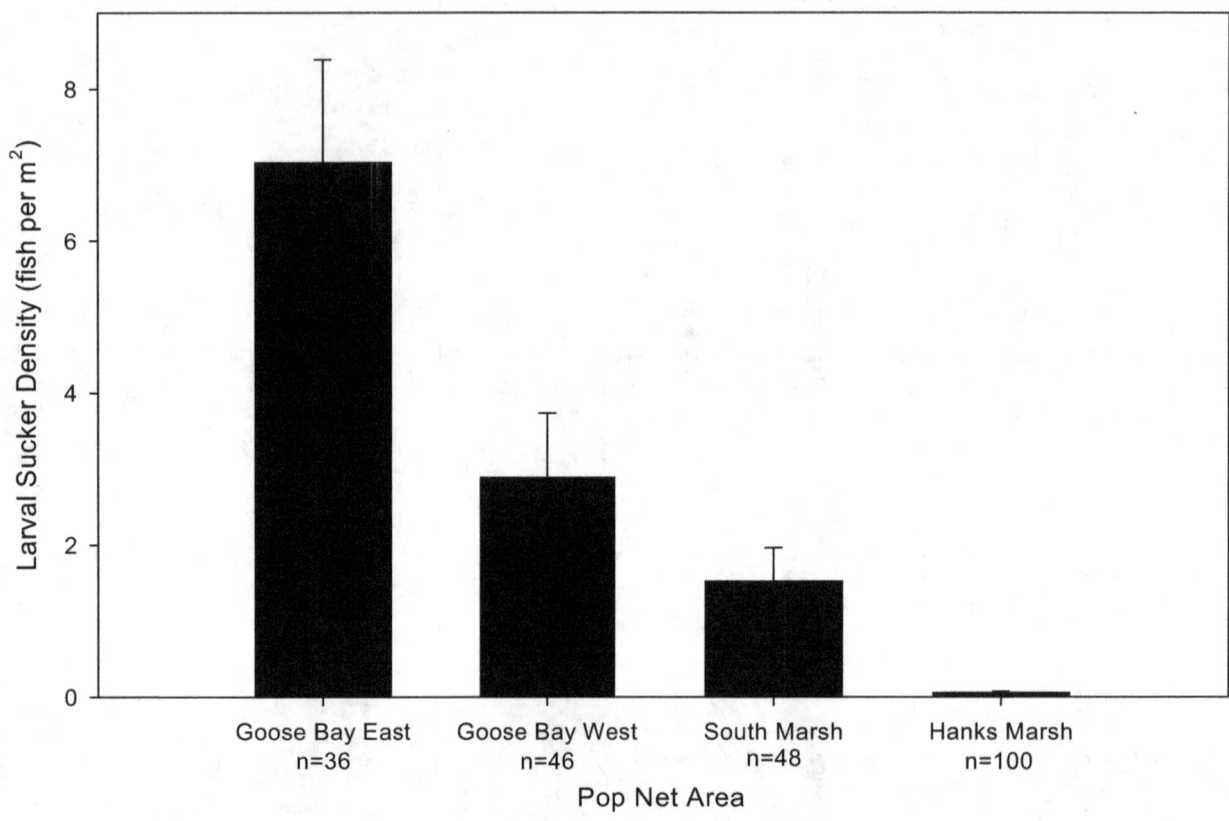

Figure 9. Comparison of mean larval sucker CPUE (larvae per m³; + 1 SE) in Hanks Marsh to mean larval sucker density at three other marsh sites in Upper Klamath Lake, Oregon, from May 14 to June 20, 2007. Data for Goose Bay and South Marsh were converted from values given in Hendrixson (2008), by dividing them by the volume that pop nets sampled assuming a 1 m depth. The total number of pop nets sampled (n) during this period is given.

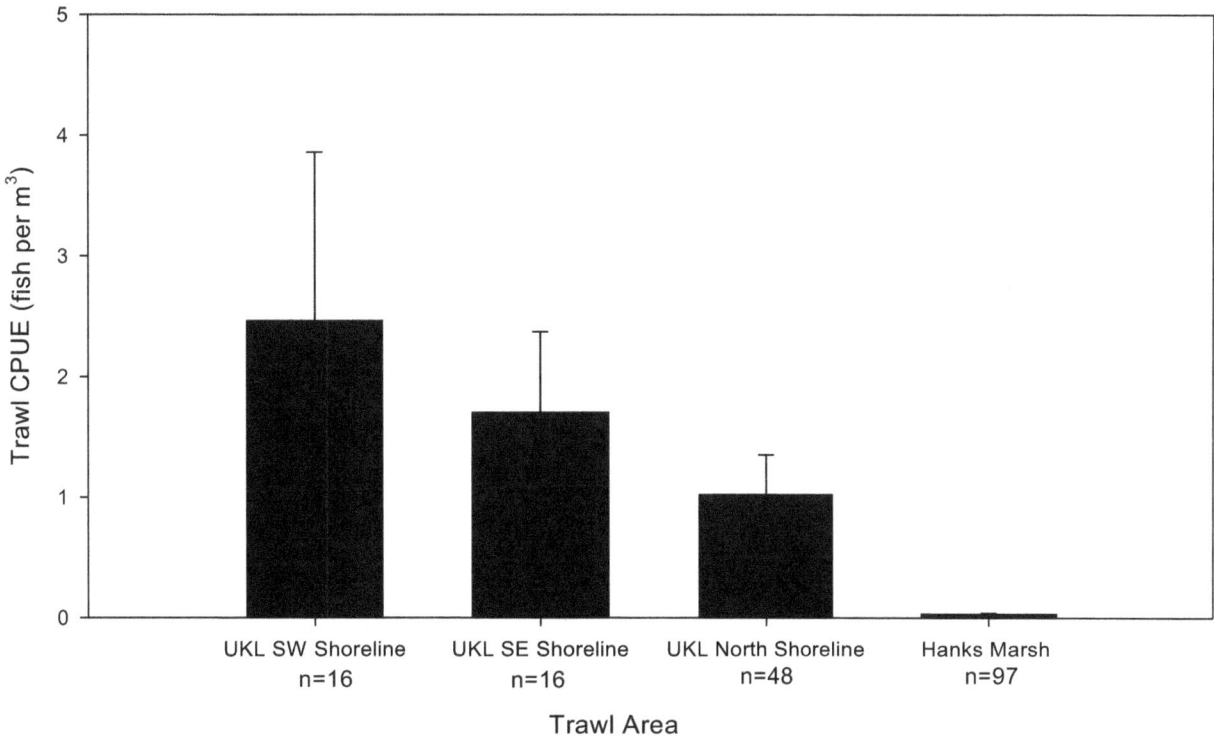

Figure 10. Comparison of mean catch per unit effort (CPUE; fish per m³; + 1 SE) for larval trawl catches at Hanks Marsh to three other nearshore areas of Upper Klamath Lake (UKL), Oregon, between May 7 and July 18, 2007. Data for the lake sites are from Simon and Markle (2008). The number of larval trawl samples collected in each area over the same period also is given.

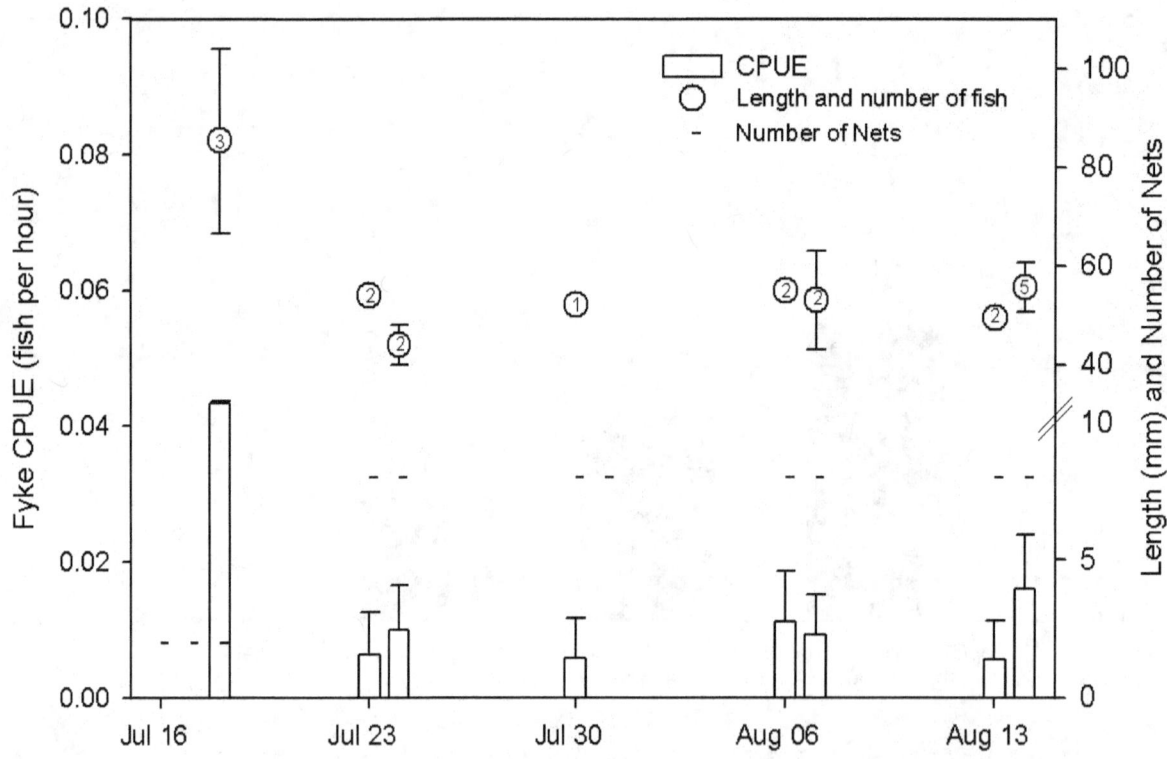

Figure 11. Mean daily catch per unit effort (CPUE; fish per hour; + 1 SE) and mean standard length (mm; ± 1 SE) for juvenile suckers captured by fyke nets in Hanks Marsh, Upper Klamath Lake, Oregon, 2007. The numbers of samples and fish used to calculate means and standard errors are given.

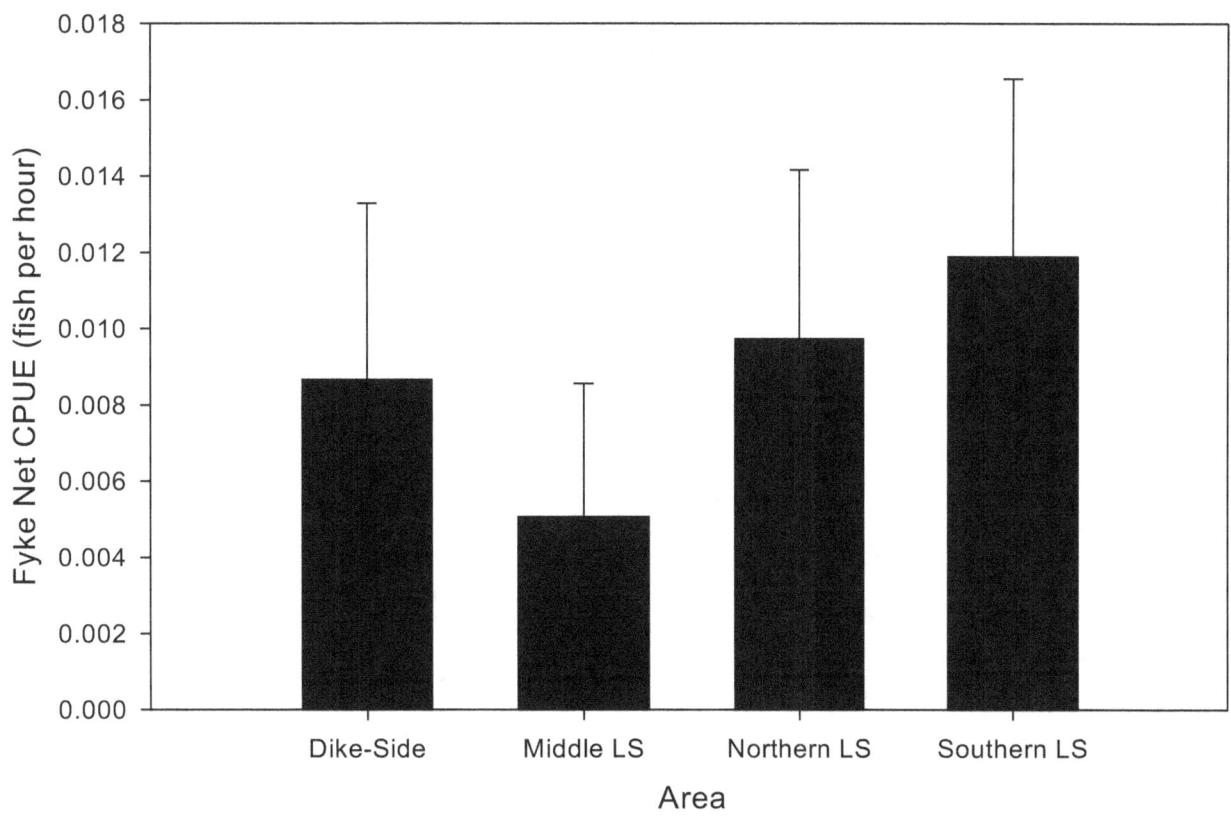

Figure 12. Mean catch per unit effort (CPUE; fish per hour; + 1 SE) for juvenile suckers caught in fyke nets along the lake-side (LS) and the dike-side of Hanks Marsh, Upper Klamath Lake, Oregon, summer 2007. The number of fyke nets set in each area is given in table 4.

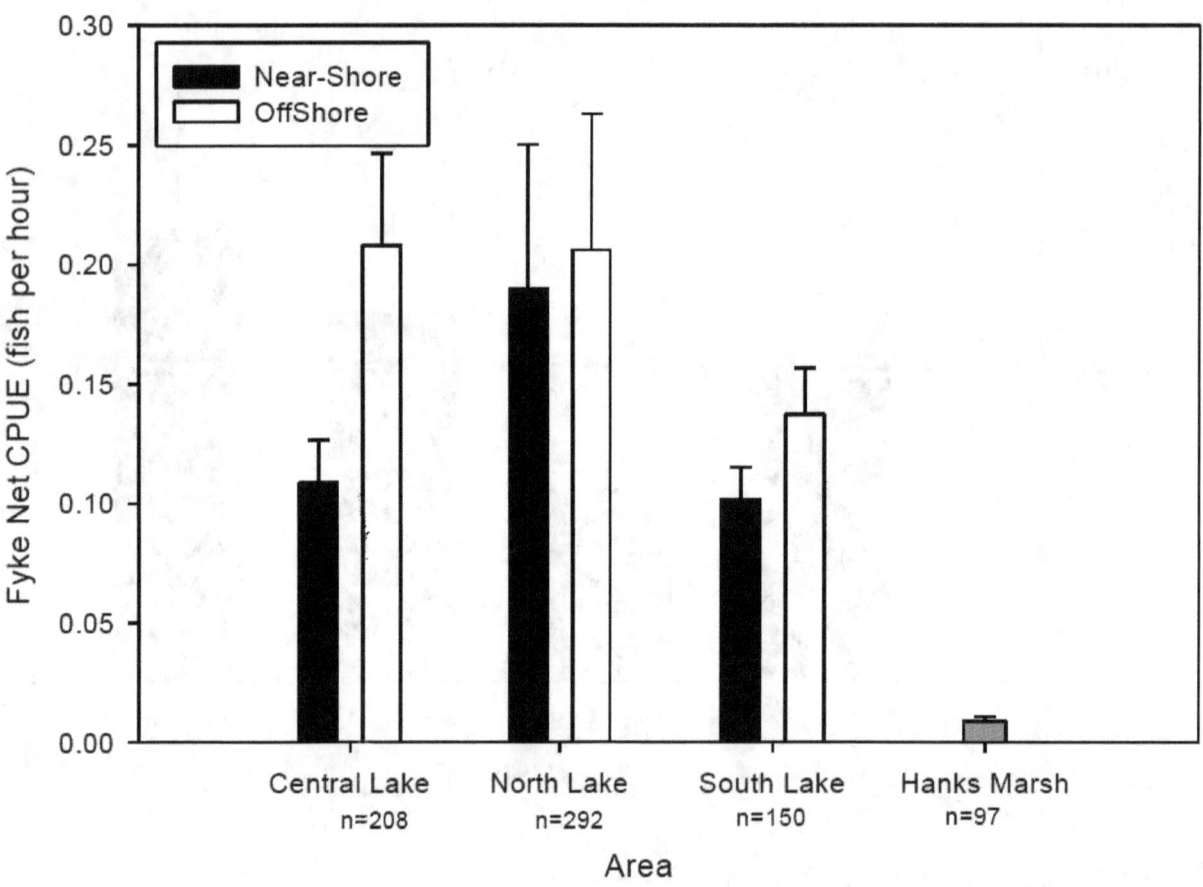

Figure 13. Mean catch per unit effort (CPUE; fish per hour; + 1 SE) for juvenile suckers caught in fyke nets set in three different areas of Upper Klamath Lake in the nearshore (<100 m from shore) and off-shore (>100 m from shore) compared with those set in Hanks Marsh between July 16 and August 14, 2007 (USGS unpublished data, 2007).

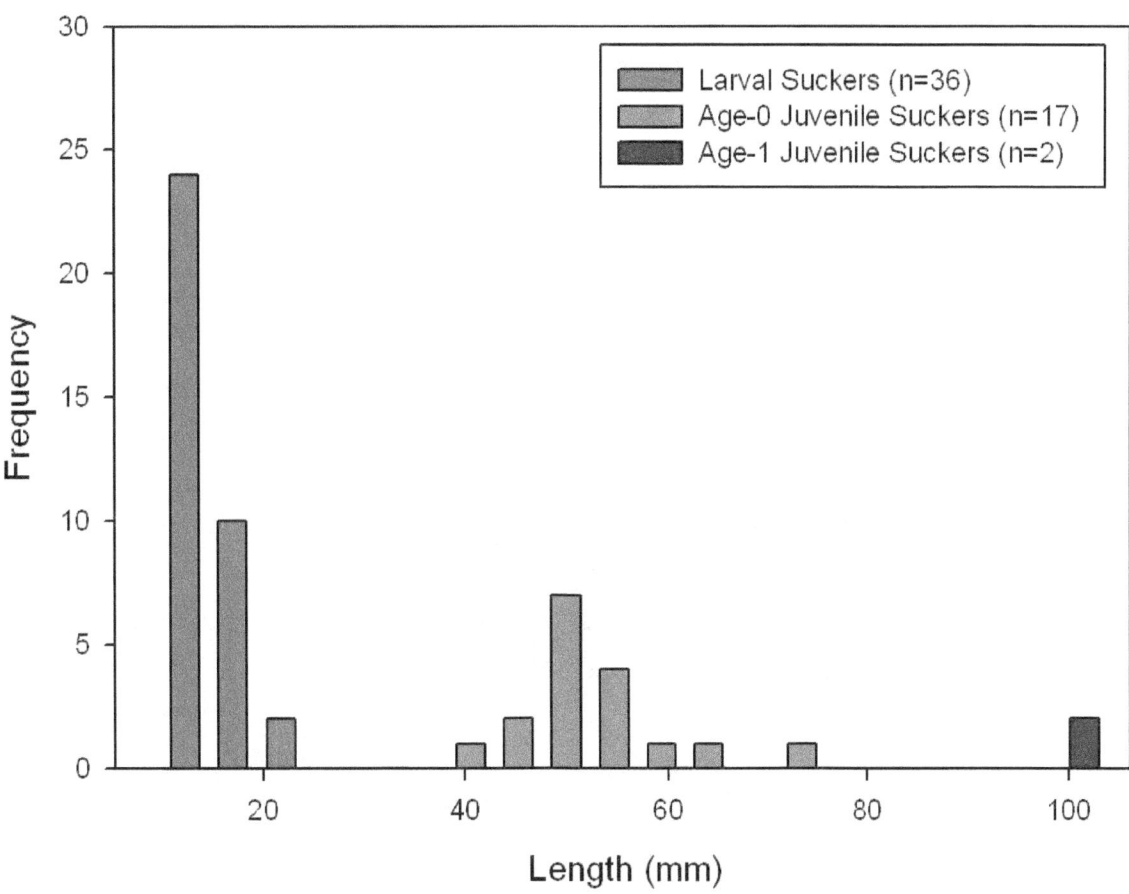

Figure 14. Length frequency distribution for suckers of three age classes caught in Hanks Marsh, Upper Klamath Lake, Oregon, 2007 using all three types of gear (pop nets, trawls, and fyke nets). Length was measured as notochord length (mm) for larval suckers and standard length (mm) for juvenile suckers. Lengths were grouped in 5-mm length bins.

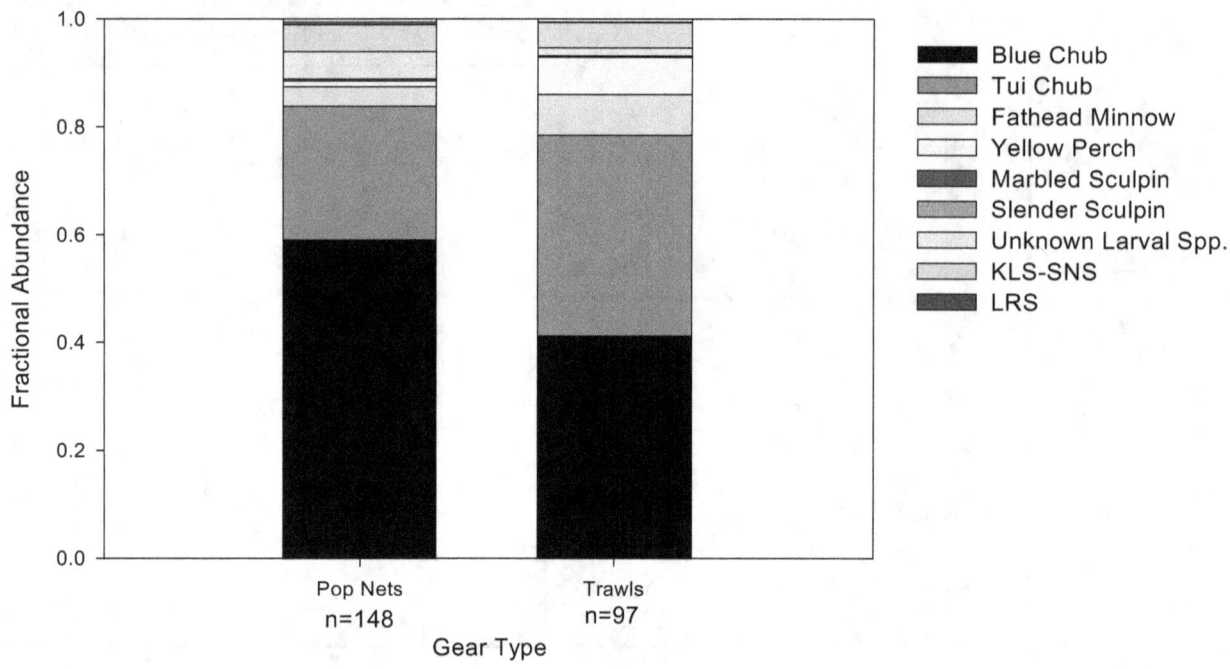

Figure 15. Proportional species composition of pop net catches and trawls at sites in Hanks Marsh, Upper Klamath Lake, Oregon, 2007. The number of samples (n) taken with each gear type also is given.

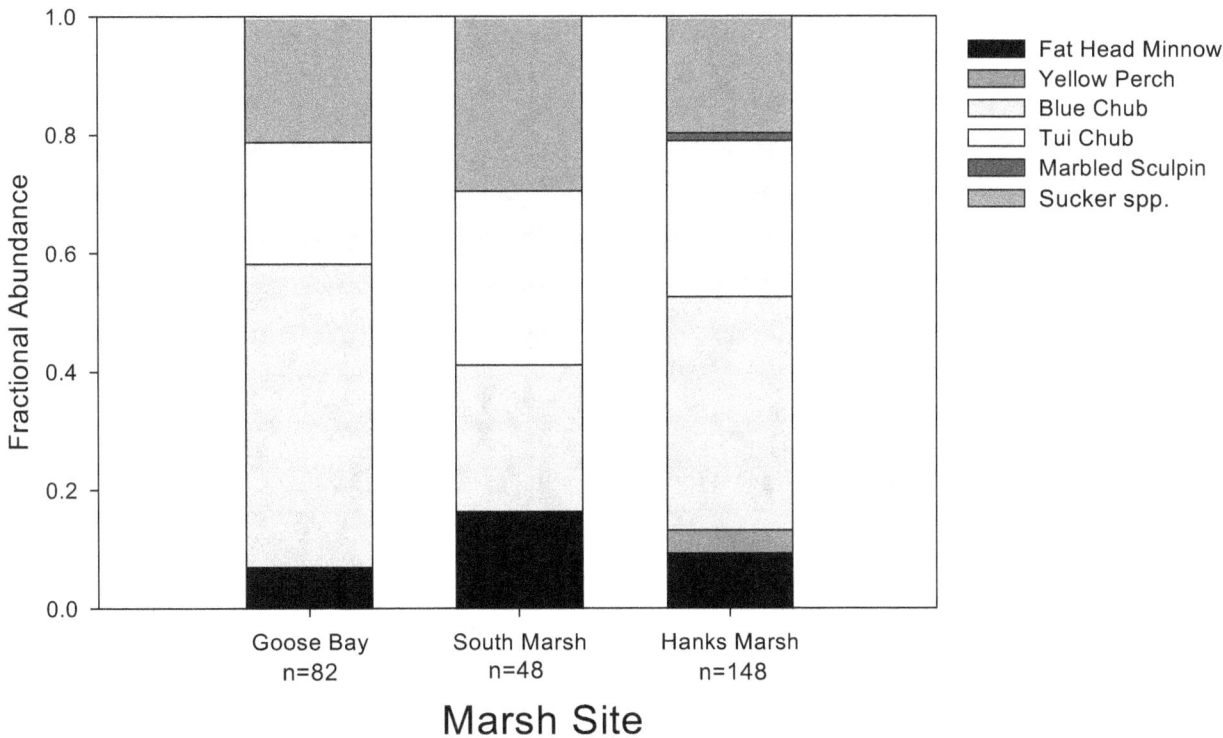

Figure 16. Comparison of proportional larval species composition in pop net catches at Hanks Marsh to those at three other marsh sites in Upper Klamath Lake, Oregon, 2007. Goose Bay and South Marsh data are from Hendrixson (2008). The numbers of nets sampled (n) in 2007 in each marsh also are given.

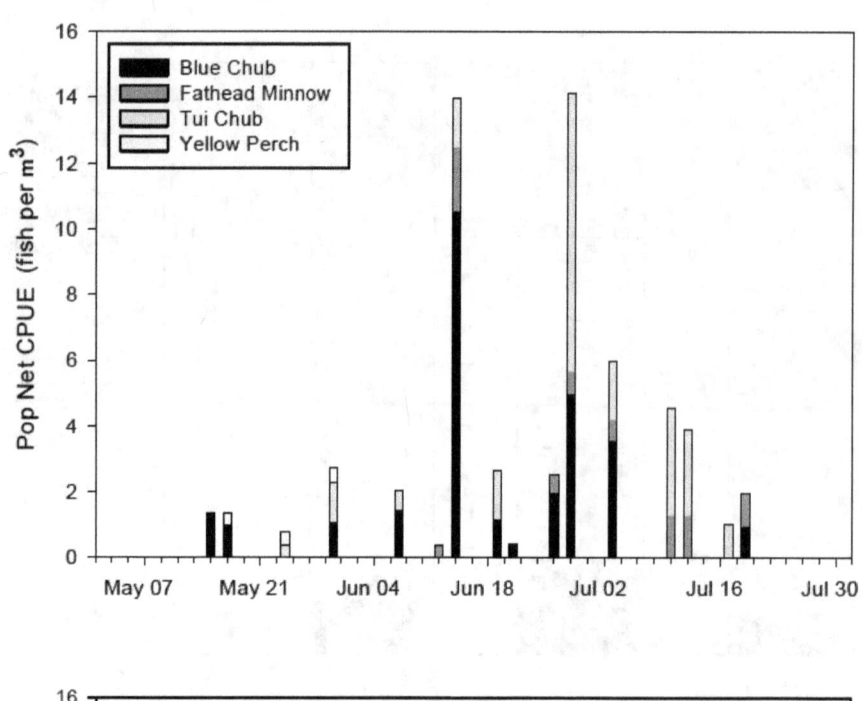

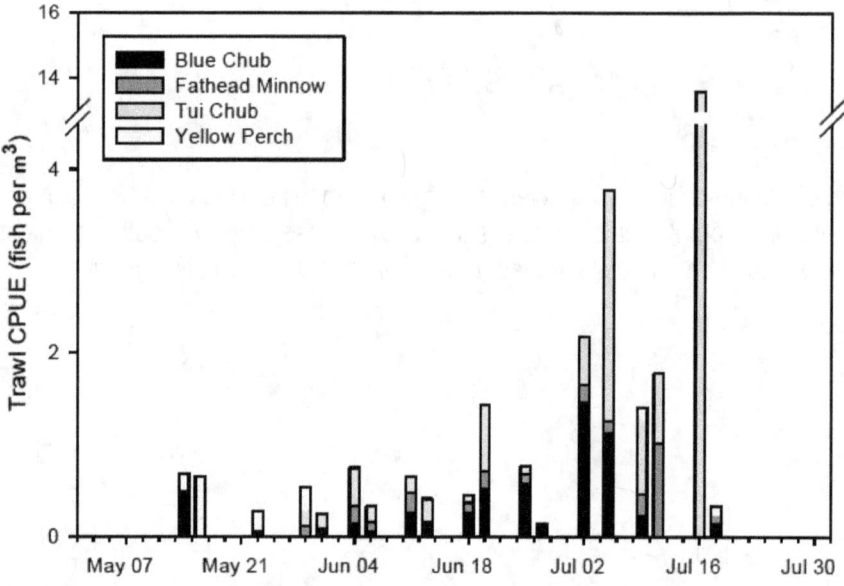

Figure 17. Mean catch per unit effort (CPUE; fish per m³) of non-sucker species for (a) pop net catches and (b) trawl net catches between April 30 and July 19 at sites in Hanks Marsh, Upper Klamath Lake, Oregon, 2007.

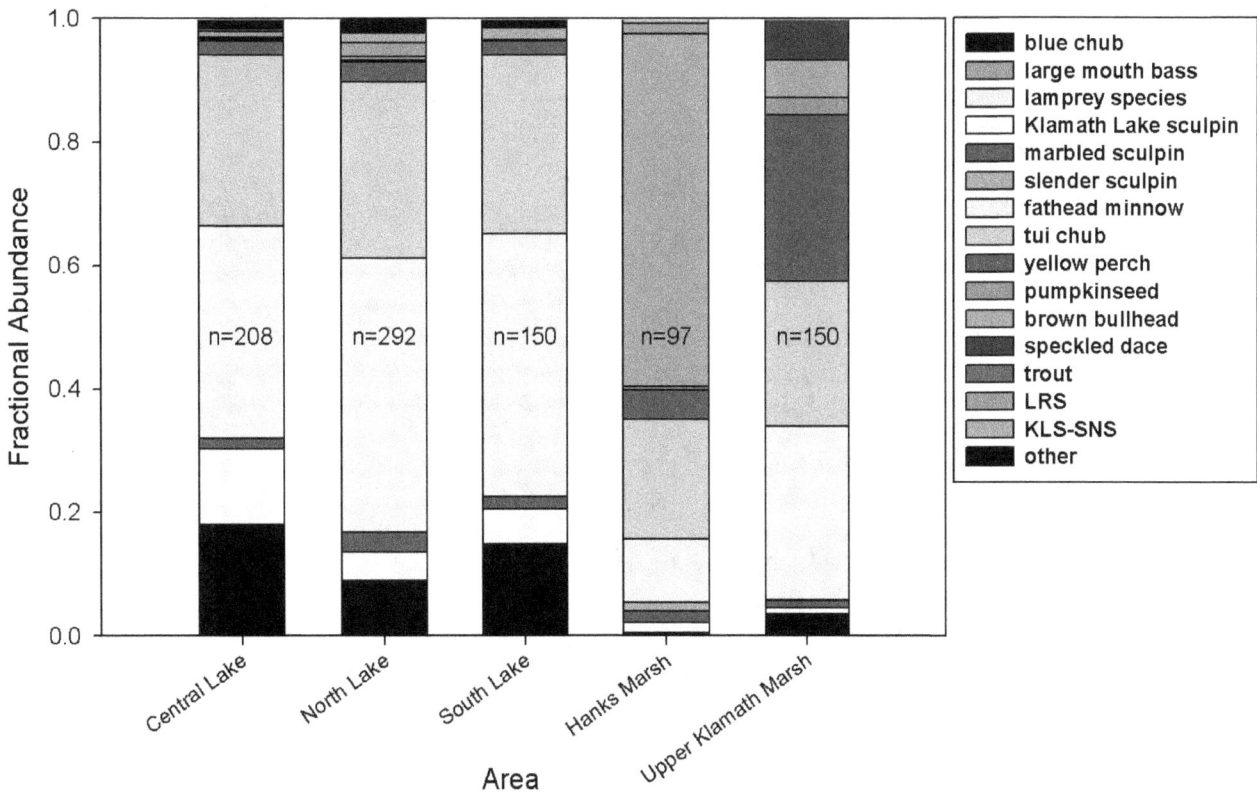

Figure 18. Proportional species composition of fyke net catches in three different areas of Upper Klamath Lake, Hanks Marsh, and Upper Klamath Marsh (Pelican Bay Unit of the Upper Klamath National Wildlife Refuge Marsh). Data for the three portions of Upper Klamath Lake (Central, North, South) are from Burdick and others (unpublished data, 2008) and data for Upper Klamath Marsh are from Mulligan and Mulligan (2007). The number of nets set in each area during this time period also is given.

Median Water Quality

Site-Specific Water Quality

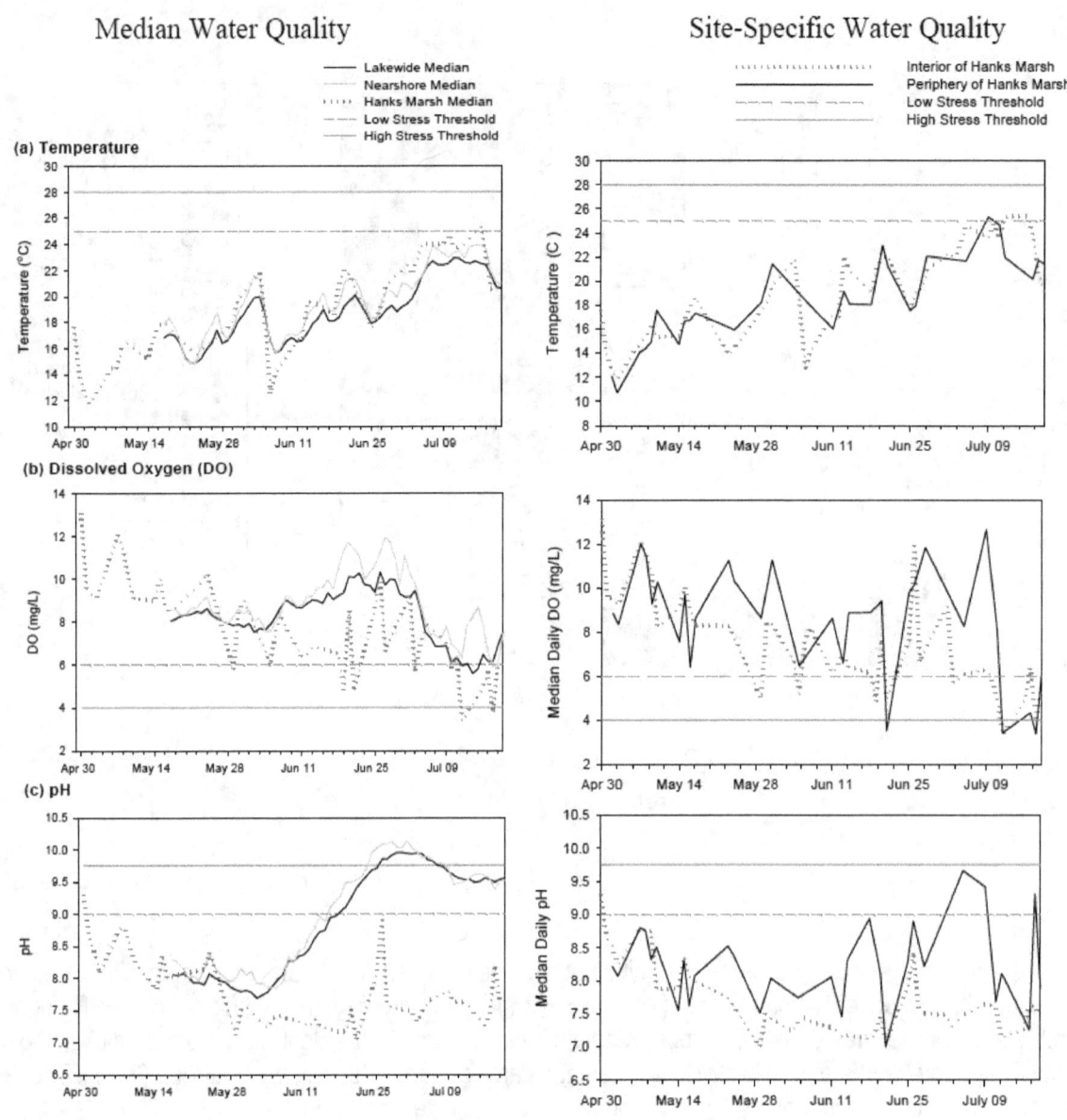

Figure 19. Recorded median temperature (a), dissolved oxygen (b), and pH (c) values from all sampling sites in Hanks Marsh, Upper Klamath Lake, Oregon, between April 30 and July 19, 2007. High and low stress threshold levels for sucker species (Loftus, 2001) are included on each plot. Daily median water-quality values also are shown from 14 lake-wide and 5 nearshore sites in Upper Klamath Lake, Oregon (M. Lindenburg, USGS, unpublished data, 2007).